AMERICAN SCHOOL OF PREHISTORIC RESEARCH

PEABODY MUSEUM · HARVARD UNIVERSITY
BULLETIN NO. 34

EXCAVATION OF THE
ABRI PATAUD
LES EYZIES (DORDOGNE)

Hallam L. Movius, Jr.
General Editor and Director of Excavations

Harvey M. Bricker
Volume Editor

THE PÉRIGORDIAN VI (LEVEL 3) ASSEMBLAGE

by
Harvey M. Bricker
and
Nicholas David

PEABODY MUSEUM OF ARCHAEOLOGY AND ETHNOLOGY
Harvard University, Cambridge, Massachusetts
1984

Distributed by Harvard University Press

Contents

Figures

Tables

Preface

The nature of this report on the Périgordian VI industries at the Abri Pataud has been strongly conditioned by the overall research design of the Pataud project (which changed and developed over the span of several decades) as well as by the vagaries of the research schedules of the co-authors and other project participants. The project director, Hallam L. Movius, Jr., has explained elsewhere (Movius 1974) that the original research design, conceived in the late 1940s and first put into practice in the early 1950s, emphasized the application of new excavation techniques to rock shelters with complex stratigraphy, the fullest possible investigation of the paleoenvironmental contexts of the occupations, and—in the realm of culture history—a detailed testing against new data of some of Denis Peyrony's interpretations of his recently proposed "Périgordian" tool-making tradition (D. Peyrony 1933, 1936). Denis Peyrony's major arguments had been stratigraphic and typological, and the new data that were expected to be relevant to those arguments were considered to be of the same kind. (The same would be true later when the research design of the Abri Pataud project was expanded to include a reexamination of Aurignacian systematics.)

By about 1960, it had become apparent that the limits of the traditional typology for French Upper Palaeolithic tools, most usefully codified by de Sonneville-Bordes and Perrot (1954–1956), were too confining for an adequate investigation of even those questions that Peyrony had posed, and certainly for any attempts to ask more anthropologically phrased questions about prehistoric cultural dynamics. A set of analytic procedures was needed to describe and manipulate the variation in stone tools that existed within the traditional types; a subtypological or attribute analysis was called for. Although at the time such an approach was not yet part of the normal methodology of French prehistorians, it was very similar to methods being developed concurrently but independently for the Hungarian Middle Palaeolithic by László Vértes (1964). Between 1960 and 1970, most of the archaeologists associated with the Abri Pataud project (Hallam Movius, Nicholas David, Harvey Bricker, Berle Clay, and Alison Brooks) devoted large portions of their time to developing attribute recording standards (Movius et al. 1968; Movius and Brooks 1971) and to collecting, through comparative study, the large bodies of comparable attribute data that were necessary to the investigation of interassemblage variability.

Four major studies that applied the newly developed analytic techniques to various Pataud assemblages and relevant samples from other Upper Palaeolithic sites were undertaken between the early 1960s and the mid-1970s (David 1966;

Clay 1968; Bricker 1973; Brooks 1979). In accord with the project director's wish to avoid a plethora of preliminary papers, only a few selected aspects of the substantive results of these studies, which were originally the doctoral dissertations of Movius's younger colleagues, have so far been published (Movius and David 1970; David 1973; Clay 1976; Bricker 1976, 1978). The Périgordian VI industry figured prominently in several of the four studies, but always as a point of comparison or a foil that permitted the clearer definition of the other industries with which their authors were primarily concerned. The present monograph is, then, a much-revised restructuring of parts of two earlier and more integrally conceived studies. As a descriptive analysis of hitherto unpublished materials from the Abri Pataud it stands independently, but as a comparative analysis it suffers, temporarily, from the discrepancy between the optimal order of publication of the archaeological results from the Abri Pataud and the order imposed by circumstances. This volume compares the Périgordian VI to the Périgordian IV (late Middle Périgordian), but Bricker's descriptive analysis of the Middle Périgordian at Pataud will be one of the later volumes in the Pataud series. The other interassemblage comparisons will appear, sooner, in volumes by Clay and David.

The Abri Pataud project's research design has another characteristic that has helped to determine the nature of this report (as well as of the archaeological volumes to be published subsequently): this is its strong compartmentalization of research effort. The Pataud project is similar in this respect to other long-term, multidisciplinary, and multinational research programs, and it has, like many of them, discovered the costs that must be paid in the trade-off between specialized analysis and integrative interpretation. The most clearly defined cost to the Pataud project is the inability, at this writing, to deal holistically with entire artifact assemblages in their total associational contexts. Although the archaeologists concentrating on attribute analysis of the tools and weapons have maintained a close collaboration, it has not been possible for them to incorporate final results of the still ongoing research on techniques of lithic *débitage* (Collins n.d.a, n.d.b) or the study of living-floor definition and the horizontal spatial patterning of artifacts (Whallon 1973, 1974; Clay 1975). Interaction between the archaeologists and the natural scientists was facilitated by a field conference held at the Abri Pataud in the summer of 1967—after the excavations were finished but in time for the archaeologists to use the results of sedimentology, and so on, in their analyses. The much more recent zooarchaeological studies of Spiess (1979) respond to questions that are of greater salience now than they were several decades ago, and we have attempted to deal in this report with those of his findings that concern the Périgordian VI.

During the past several decades, the co-authors have accumulated debts of gratitude to many persons who have facilitated their research in various ways. First among those whose aid they are happy to acknowledge is Hallam L. Movius, Jr., the Director of Excavations of the Harvard Dordogne Project and the director of their doctoral studies. They are grateful for his permission to study the Périgordian VI and other collections from the Abri Pataud, for making available to them the facilities of the Abri Pataud laboratory and the results of the work of other expedition staff members (especially the superb artifact illustrations of Pierre Laurent), for financial support of their work on several occasions, and for his encouragement and advice. They extend a warm thanks as well to Nancy Movius, who, in many ways over many years, facilitated the smooth working of the expedition, kept their time free for the research they were in France to do, and was, in general, an unfailing friend.

The National Science Foundation has generously awarded Harvard University a publication grant, BNS-7912955, to cover the expenses of this volume. In addition, the co-authors acknowledge with gratitude the financial support each received from National Science Foundation Dissertation Improvement Grants. Among the many who contributed to the execution of their research on the Périgordian VI, they wish to thank, in particular, the following:

Jean Guichard, Conservateur du Musée National des Eyzies, and Elie Peyrony, the former Conservateur, for permission to examine the materials from Laugerie-Haute-Est: B and B';

R. Berle Clay, for helpful discussions over a period of several years about Upper Périgordian backed tools;

William R. Farrand, for his aid, in discussion and correspondence, in understanding the geochronological sequence of the Abri Pataud;

Gregory Scott, for his aid in the final typing of portions of the manuscript; and

Lorna Condon, Editor for the Peabody Museum, and Kate Bennett, Copy Editor, for their help and patience in the execution of a difficult task.

Finally, the co-authors would like to offer a special word of thanks to the people of the Périgord among whom they lived for so many years, including the people of the *communes* of Les Eyzies and Tursac, especially the Bouyssou and Lisiak families of Lespinasse. The importance to the research program of the friendship and cooperation that these people offered can be neither precisely measured nor overstated.

Harvey M. Bricker
Department of Anthropology
Tulane University
New Orleans, Louisiana 70118
U.S.A.

Nicholas David
Department of Archaeology
University of Calgary
Calgary, Alberta T2N 1N4
Canada

Excavation of the
Abri Pataud

The Périgordian VI (Level 3): Introduction

THE SETTLEMENT AND THE ENVIRONMENT

What is referred to globally as the Level 3 occupation at the Abri Pataud is in fact the record of several successive, discontinuous occupations of the rock shelter by prehistoric people making Périgordian VI artifacts. The stratigraphic information previously published by Movius (1977) documents the presence of at least four, and probably as many as six, separate Périgordian VI occupational episodes in that part of the shelter sampled by the excavation program.

Evidence of the first Périgordian VI occupation at the site occurs in the 3-cm- to 15-cm-thick Level 3: Lens 4 in one part of the site (Movius 1977, pp. 44, 45) and in the contemporaneous sediments at the base of what is called Eboulis 3-4: Yellow in other parts of the site (ibid., pp. 54, 55). Little is known of this occupation because it was apparently centered to the north of the excavated area (north of Trench VI; cf. ibid., fig.2). It is clear, however, that it dates to the very beginning of the cold, dry climatic episode (Farrand 1975, p. 63) during which all Périgordian VI occupation of the Abri Pataud occurred. Lens 4 and an outlying pile of river-stones in Trench VI, a small ashy lens in Trench IV, and a scatter of burnt bone in Trench III all lie directly on the weathered surface of Eboulis 3-4: Red, sediments representing the previous warm, moist episode. The basin containing Hearth F of Lens 4 is dug into Eboulis 3-4: Red (Movius 1977, fig.6). Cultural remains from this earliest occupation include: the basined hearth itself, other discrete ash concentrations, and a generally high ash content in the Lens 4 sediment; a small sample of retouched flint tools and evidence of tool manufacture at the site (unretouched *débitage* products and 11 nuclei); a concentrated pile of river-stones adjacent to Hearth F; some sparse faunal material, some of it burnt; and traces of red ochre. These remains, distributed along 10 linear m in the rear of the shelter, suggest that the excavations sampled the southern fringe of what was a major occupational episode.

The remains of the second Périgordian VI occupation, located again in the rear of the shelter, are separated from those of the first by 5 to 8 cm of sterile sediment, Level 3: Eboulis c' (ibid., p. 44); this is a lower zone of what is called Eboulis 3-4: Yellow in the front of the shelter, where occupational traces are absent. The occupation horizon is a 5-cm-thick body of red-stained sediment; it is designated Level 3: Lens 3 (ibid.) and is located in Trenches V and VI. Its cultural contents include: a localized ash spread (but not a basined hearth) in Trench V; a few retouched flint tools and some *débitage* flakes; numerous river-stones; some faunal remains, many of which are fish bones; and a small cobble, used at some time as a flaking tool, bearing the engraved representations of several animal (horse?) heads. These data suggest that the second occupation, like the first, was centered to the north of Trench VI and that the excavations sampled, in approximately 4 linear m, only a small portion of its southern fringe.

The second occupation was followed, at least in the excavated area, by an interval of unknown duration during which little or no occupation took place. Level 3: Lens 3 is directly overlain by Level 3: Eboulis c, an 8- to 10-cm-thick body of nearly sterile sediment (ibid.) It was approximately during this same interval of time that the line of large roof blocks (cf. ibid., fig. 12) that were to become so important for subsequent Périgordian VI occupations fell to the floor of the shelter. The stratigraphic data available do not allow us to demonstrate an exact contemporaneity between the roof-collapse events and the deposition of Level 3: Eboulis c, but it is clear that the collapse occurred after much of Eboulis 3-4: Yellow had already accumulated but before its deposition was completed (ibid., figs. 3, 4, 5, 14). Whatever may have been the precise sequence of events, the third and subsequent Périgordian VI occupations of the Abri Pataud took place in a shelter whose floor had a topography much different from that present during at least the first occupation. It is quite probable, in light of the later patterns of use of the shelter, that these topographic changes were in large part responsible for the southward shift in the center of the occupation zone.

Evidence of Périgordian VI occupation at the Abri Pataud continues in the thick (averaging 20 to 25 cm), archaeologically rich Level 3: Lens 2, the locus of what Movius (ibid., pp. 37–44) designates the "Main Occupation." Exactly how many discrete occupational episodes Lens 2 represents cannot be specified because "except for a few microlenses of buff-colored éboulis, no visible subdivisions were detected in the Lens 2 horizon" (ibid., p. 38). Despite the impossibility of subdividing the deposit during excavation, a number of other stratigraphic data recorded suggest the presence of at least three occupational episodes within Lens 2; these are discussed below as the third, fourth, and fifth Périgordian VI occupations of the shelter.

Many of the traces of the third occupation may have been removed or disturbed by later activities. Those that remain occur at the very base of Lens 2 and lie directly on the top of Eboulis 3-4: Yellow. These include the small, intact, non-basined Hearth E in Trenches V and VI, as well as, in Trench VI, what were interpreted as "several small hearths at the base of Lens 2 which had become scattered and subsequently covered over by debris of the Lens 2 occupation'' (ibid.). Another feature that can be attributed to this initial Lens 2 occupation is "a very concentrated lens of red, almost pure powdered hematite" (ibid., p. 40) that is 2- to 3-cm-thick and lies south of the hearths and behind the line of roof-fall blocks in Trenches II through V (ibid., figs. 6, 12). Two separate concentrations of reindeer teeth from the base of Lens 2 in Trench II (ibid., pp. 42, 43, pl. 29) may also represent this occupation. These meager data suggest that the center of the occupation, defined by the location of hearths, had shifted somewhat southward.

The fourth occupation, represented by the middle of Level 3: Lens 2, is the archaeologically richest and most complex Périgordian VI occupation encountered in the excavated area. It is distinguished from the preceding occupation not by the intercalation of sterile sediments, but rather by a further southward displacement of the locus of occupation, stratigraphic superposition, and its association with a partly natural, partly artificial "long-house" structure. This feature, previously described in detail by Movius (ibid., pp. 43, 44, fig. 12), consisted of a habitation area more than 6 m long lying between the back wall of the shelter and the upper parts of the line of roof-fall blocks located approximately 1.5 m in front (west) of the back wall. The line of closely spaced and/or overlapping blocks formed the front limit of the structure, and its height had been artificially increased, at least in places, by the construction of a (presumably low) wall of much smaller limestone blocks. The northern and southern ends of the structure were defined by differences in floor level, nature of the sediment, and differences in artifact concentrations. To the south, just beyond the probable entrance to the structure, the living floor sloped up to connect with a passageway that ran through the line of blocks and led to the mouth of the shelter. To the north, the floor sloped down sharply approximately 20 cm to an area rich in nuclei, *débitage* flakes, and dispersed ash scatter (these materials may be refuse from the structure).

Although discrete episodes cannot be identified, it is clear that occupation within the "long-house" structure took place over an extended period. Two hearths, C and D, date to the early part of the "long-house" occupation. The base of Hearth C lay just above the hematite lens of the third occupation, and the excavated basin of Hearth D probably cut through the hematite into Eboulis 3-4: Yellow. The filling of Hearth C consisted of "a series of thin ash layers alternating with barely perceptible, very thin lenses of buff-colored éboulis" (ibid., p. 40), an indication of successive episodes of reuse. Hearth B, the third hearth within the limits of the "long-house" structure, dates to somewhat later in that occupation. It was located near, but not at the top of, Lens 2, and its ash scatter overlay that of Hearth C. This fourth or "long-house" occupation of the shelter provided the major portion of the Périgordian VI archaeological material recovered in the excavations.

The fifth Périgordian VI occupation is represented by archaeological material from the very top of Level 3: Lens 2, near the southern edge of the excavated area in Trenches I and II, outside the limits of the earlier "long-house" structure. There is, indeed, good evidence that the "long-house" structure no longer existed in its original form at the time of the fifth occupation. Concentrations of stones interpreted as fallen portions of the low wall built earlier atop the line of roof-fall blocks were found in several places in Trenches II through V in the upper part of Lens 2 (ibid., pp. 41, 42). The fifth occupation was centered on Hearth A, a basined hearth that had originally been dug into Lens 2 from its upper surface and had been subsequently reused several times. By the time Hearth A was used, therefore, the "long-house" structure had fallen into ruin; its former floor was covered with some depth of rubble, and the line of roof-fall blocks must have provided diminished protection from the mouth of the rock shelter. Another possible trace of the fifth occupation is a diffuse concentration of chipping debris in Trench II; it was adjacent to and apparently just above the surface of Hearth A. The concentration, which contained 345 *débitage* flakes of the same flint variety, probably represents the somewhat disturbed results of one knapping episode (ibid., pp. 43, 44). Other archaeological materials from the summit of Lens 2 are sparse.

An interruption in the Périgordian VI occupation of the Abri Pataud once again ensued. With the deposition of 8 to 30 cm of the virtually sterile Level 3: Eboulis b (ibid., p. 36), the tops of the line of roof-fall blocks were buried, and the last traces of the "long-house"-structure topography disappeared.

Material from the sixth and final Périgordian VI occupation of the Abri Pataud occurred in Level 3: Lens 1 and the immediately overlying scatter of cultural material designated Level 3: Eboulis a. Lens 1, a darkly stained sediment averaging 3 to 4 cm in thickness, did not contain a discrete hearth, but it was full of ash and burnt bone. Debris from this final occupation included over 100 retouched tools and numerous *débitage* flakes, bone and antler refuse, and some broken river-stones. The locus of this occupation had shifted back somewhat to the north, being centered in Trenches II and III (ibid., figs. 3, 4, 14), but scattered traces of occupation were found elsewhere on the shelter's floor (e.g., hematite fragments and staining as far north as Trench VI).

Use of the Abri Pataud by people making Périgordian VI tools ended with the Lens 1/Eboulis a occupation. Deposition of sterile éboulis fragments under conditions of frost weathering continued under the overhang and in front of it (Farrand 1975), resulting in the accumulation of the 20-to-25-cm-thick Eboulis 2-3: Light Reddish Brown. Cultural debris is virtually absent from this level, except in the front of the shelter, where its precise stratigraphic relationship with the occupation area under the overhang is not known. After a brief mild climatic episode during which soil formation started in the Eboulis 2-3: Light Reddish Brown sediments, a new and more severe climatic episode started with a roof-fall and continued with severe frost weathering (ibid.). It was early in this new period of cold, dry climate responsible for the deposition of Eboulis 2-3 that the first sporadic traces of reoccupation of the Abri Pataud appear; the few artifacts available from this time period are typical of the Proto-Magdalenian tool-making tradition abundantly represented in the overlying Level 2 (Movius 1975, p. 30).

The several Périgordian VI occupations discussed above make very unequal contributions to the pooled sample of artifacts that is treated here, for purposes of typological analysis, as a unitary "Level 3 assemblage." Over 90% (approximately 1,900) of the retouched tools and nuclei in the pooled assemblage-sample are from Lens 2 (Movius 1977, p. 38). Because consistent stratigraphic subdivision of this deposit during excavation was not possible, the artifacts from the third, fourth, and fifth occupations are not separately identifiable, but the gross stratigraphic and lateral distributional evidence summarized above makes it clear that most of these tools are associated with the fourth or "long-house" occupation. The sixth and last occupation contributed just over 100 tools and nuclei to the Level 3 assemblage (ibid., p. 36). The earliest occupations, both centered to the north of the area excavated, contributed little to the assemblage sample. The first contributed approximately 30 tools and nuclei (ibid., pp. 45, 54); the second contributed approximately 23 (ibid., p. 44). The unretouched *débitage* products (utilized blades, chipping debris, and so on) from Level 3 and other levels at the Abri Pataud are the subject of a separate study still in process; they are not included in the artifact totals and are not considered further here.

The fullest information about environmental conditions during the several Périgordian VI occupations of the Abri Pataud is provided by the sedimentological study of Farrand (1975). The record of climatic change is not as closely tied to the detailed archaeological succession as one might wish because by the time Farrand joined the research project and started sample collection (1964 and 1965), those areas of the site in which the Périgordian VI stratigraphic succession was most completely represented had been removed by excavation (in 1958 and 1959). All three of Farrand's columns that sampled the Périgordian VI (his columns AP2, AP3, and AP4) did so in areas where there was minimal internal stratigraphic differentiation. Despite this fact, however, both earlier and later stages of the occupation were sampled unambiguously, and the results of sedimentology are generally quite clear.

A sequence of six successive Périgordian VI occupations has been discussed above. The general time span during and immediately after which the first two of these occurred—Level 3: Lens 4 though Level 3: Eboulis c—is sampled by Farrand's samples AP2-8 and AP3-6. That the stratigraphic assignment for both is given as Eboulis 3-4: Yellow (ibid., p. 34, pl. 1) should not obscure the fact that they represent the time of the earliest Level 3 occupation. It will be recalled that only in the extreme rear of the shelter were occupational remains dense enough to permit stratigraphic differentiation; the contemporaneous sediments further toward the front—including Square E, where columns AP2 and AP3 were located—were designated Eboulis 3-4: Yellow.

The third Périgordian VI occupation, the few remaining traces of which were located some meters distant from the standing section-walls available to Farrand, was very probably not sampled by him.

The time of the fourth occupation—that associated with the "long-house" structure—is almost certainly represented by Farrand's sample AP3-5. Although Level 3 was not stratigraphically differentiated here, other evidence (summarized above) indicates that the sediment in question was that containing the scatter of cultural debris extending north and northwest from the northern end of the "long-house."

Farrand's sample AP2-7, from the undifferentiated "passageway" deposits leading to the mouth of the shelter, must be assigned globally to the "later" Périgordian VI occupations. It almost certainly samples the time of the fourth occupation, and probably those of the fifth and sixth also. The period of the shelter's abandonment between the sixth Périgordian VI and the first Proto-Magdalenian occupations is represented by Farrand's samples AP2-5, AP2-6, AP3-4, and AP4-3, all from Eboulis 2-3: Light Reddish Brown.

In light of these data, the climatic sequence revealed by sedimentology may be briefly summarized as follows: People making Périgordian VI tools first occupied the Abri Pataud coincident with the beginning of an episode of cold, dry climate—a climate that continued throughout the whole sequence of Périgordian VI occupations. Early in this period, a major rock-fall from the shelter roof transformed the topography of the living area in such a way as to make possible the "long-house" structure of the fourth occupation. By the end of the Périgordian VI occupational sequence, and perhaps increasingly immediately after it, the cold climate with abundant freeze-thaw cycles became more humid. This climate gave way to a "brief mild episode with incipient pedogenesis" (Farrand 1975, p. 63), which was followed, in turn, by a return of the severe cold evidenced by Eboulis 2-3, containing the first Proto-Magdalenian tools. What is most important for intersite geochronological comparisons (discussed further below) is the fact that all the Périgordian VI occupations at the Abri Pataud are found in cold-climate sediments; by the time of significant climatic amelioration (represented by the weathering of Eboulis 2-3: Light Reddish Brown), people making Périgordian VI tools had long since ceased to inhabit the Abri Pataud.

For reasons explained by Donner (1975, p. 167), the study of pollen from the Abri Pataud sediments has made a disappointingly small contribution to the understanding of climatic change as revealed by changes in the nearby floral communities. No palynological data are available for the early Périgordian VI occupations, and a single, very small sample (33 pollen grains) represents the later occupations. Donner's diagnosis of the Level 3 sample as representing a "forest steppe with *Betula, Pinus,* and *Quercus* mainly in sheltered parts of the valleys" (ibid., p. 170, table 2) seems to be generally consistent with the sedimentological information.

Faunal material from Level 3 provides additional corroborative evidence about the climate of the period. The study of the vertebrate fauna by Bouchud (1975) offers little information about the climate of the first two Périgordian VI occupations because he was unable to make a separation

4 ABRI PATAUD: PÉRIGORDIAN VI (LEVEL 3) ASSEMBLAGE

between materials from Eboulis 3-4: Red (Noaillian) and materials from Eboulis 3-4: Yellow (Périgordian VI). The data are, however, much fuller for the later occupations; the faunal sample was analyzed globally, but most of it comes from Lens 2 and thus represents the third, fourth, and fifth occupations. Reindeer, which account for over 90% (by count) of the sample, provide only rather generalized climatic information, and Bouchud depends on some of the less frequently represented species for more detailed information. The presence of species now living in high mountains indicates a rigorously cold climate and a general lowering of snow line during Level 3 times. The mountain species in question are ibex, chamois, and three birds (ptarmigan, bearded vulture, and Alpine chough). The presence in quantity of aurochs and/or bison (37% by count of the nonreindeer mammalian sample) indicates sufficient humidity to permit the extensive presence of the requisite forest-steppe environments, and the nearly equal frequency of horse (34%) is taken as a further indication of steppe habitats (ibid., p. 144). The environmental complexity suggested by the paleontology is in accord with the results of palynology.

Two different studies of the Level 3 faunal sample have provided information about the seasonality of the Périgordian VI occupations. Bouchud (1975) obtained his data on seasonality by estimating the month of death of reindeer based on regularities in dental development and antler growth. Spiess (1979) derived similar information from (1) reindeer dental development, (2) a study of tooth cementum growth rings in reindeer, aurochs, and horse, and (3) estimates of time of availability of salmon in the Vézère River. Because Bouchud's sample was limited to Lens 2 and later units of Level 3, and Speiss's sample to Lens 2 only, there is no direct evidence for seasonality in the first two Périgordian VI occupations. Spiess's work with other levels at the Abri Pataud suggests, however, that the pattern of seasonal use of the rock shelter remained very stable (ibid., p. 194, table 6.5), and the seasonality of the later Périgordian VI occupations is unlikely to be different from that of the earlier ones.

Although Spiess is sharply critical of the techniques used by Bouchud to determine the month of death of reindeer (ibid., pp. 70–72, 97), it is happily the case that the *results* of the two seasonality studies of the Level 3 fauna are quite similar, in spite of the different techniques used. (The essential agreement of the two studies is seen only in a detailed item-by-item comparison of the relevant data, not in summary statements given by the two authors.) There is complete agreement that the Périgordian VI people occupied the Abri Pataud during the fall, winter, and spring months. Bouchud finds no evidence, and Spiess no very good evidence, that Périgordian VI occupation occurred during the midsummer months of July and August. The differences in the results of the studies are primarily ones of degree: how late in the spring (late April or late March) did Périgordian VI people leave the Abri Pataud for their summer site(s) and how early in the fall (late August or a month or so later) did they return? The documentation of the fact that the Pataud shelter comprised

just one component of a multicomponent settlement pattern of nonsedentary hunter-gatherers is important not only to attempts to understand late Périgordian use of southwest France but also to expectations about group size at seasonally occupied sites like the Abri Pataud.

Additional paleontological data adduced by Spiess (ibid.) for his Level 3: Lens 2 sample provide inferential information about the hunting practices of the Périgordian VI people. Although reindeer appear to have been the most commonly taken prey, providing appoximately 40% of the live weight killed for the Lens 2 occupations (ibid., p. 214, table 6.13, p. 215, table 6.14), the relatively small number of documented kills—40 reindeer of a total MNI (minimum number of individuals) of 58 animals of all species in the sample studied—argues against the use of large-scale drives by large groups of hunters (ibid., p. 203). The age structure of the reindeer sample from Lens 2 does not differ significantly at the .05 level from that of the modern Nelchina herd of wild caribou in Alaska (ibid., p. 193, table 6.4, p. 201, table 6.9), suggesting to Spiess that "a total population sample was available to the hunters" (ibid., p. 201) and that "the hunting methods used were not selective of age or sex" (ibid.). Given these data, Spiess suggests further that the hunting methods most likely to have been employed are "thrusting or throwing spear from ambush, stalking by single or small groups of hunters, or self-acting traps like snares, pitfalls, or nets which, to a great degree are nonselective according to age and sex" (ibid., p. 203). The use of thrusting or throwing spears is particularly likely in view of the prominence in the artifact assemblages of both flint and osseous weapon armatures.

Using a chain of argumentation based on species MNIs, meat and fat yields for those species, and human nutritional requirements, Spiess attempted to estimate population size or duration of occupation for Level 3: Lens 2 (for a given postulated population size, duration of occupation may be calculated, and vice versa). According to Spiess, the faunal refuse in his sample would have provided an estimated 2,593 man-days of occupation (ibid., p. 206); he offered the "speculation" that the Lens 2 "long-house" structure might, for example, have been occupied by approximately seven individuals during two winter seasons of six months each (1979, p. 207, fn 8). This very small estimate of both population size and occupation duration is corroborated, in Spiess's opinion, by similarities in the ratio of the number of lithic artifacts produced to the number of man-days of occupation between the Abri Pataud and a Dorset Eskimo site in Labrador (ibid., pp. 222, 223).

Although the population size during any Périgordian VI occupation—including those of Lens 2—was certainly small, Spiess's estimate of man-days of occupation was just as certainly much too low. Quite apart from problems with his choice of analytic techniques and the validity of Upper Palaeolithic-Eskimo analogies, two of his basic assumptions are inaccurate for Level 3: Lens 2. The assumptions are: (a) "the 1,700 lithics recovered are most of the lithics that found their way into archaeological context from this occupation" (ibid., p. 206); and (b) "the minimum number of individuals detected [in the faunal refuse from Trenches I through VI, Squares E, F, and G] is close to the number actually brought back to the sites" (ibid.). With respect to the first assumption, it should be pointed out that the 1,700 lithics alluded to include retouched tools and nuclei only; unretouched but utilized or unmodified *débitage* products, which were not catalogued, must be added to the tool and nucleus sample in order to obtain the total number of lithic artifacts from the Lens 2 occupations that found their way into archaeological context within the shelter itself. Results of the study of the unretouched *débitage* products from Level 3 are not yet available, but data from other levels at the Abri Pataud suggest that unretouched *débitage* products outnumber retouched tools and nuclei eight- to twelvefold. Thus the 1,700 retouched tools and nuclei considered by Spiess imply the presence of over 14,000 Lens 2 lithic artifacts within the rock shelter itself. Moreover, in a rock shelter like the Abri Pataud, a significant proportion of the cultural debris from any given occupation within the shelter finds its way into archaeological context in the talus slope deposits immediately beyond the mouth of the rock shelter. The number of Lens 2 lithic artifacts that ended up in the talus cannot be closely estimated, however, because at the time of excavation, all Level 3 talus in front of the area where Lens 2 was located had been removed by erosion and/or nineteenth-century road-building activities. That some Périgordian VI occupations of the shelter contributed artifact-rich cultural debris to the talus is, however, certain: a talus level containing Périgordian VI artifacts was found, in its expected stratigraphic position, in Test Pits N, Q, and U, which were 15 to 20 m south of the area of the Lens 2 occupation (Movius 1977, p. 153).

Similar considerations argue that the faunal refuse from Level 3: Lens 2 is significantly more copious than the sample studied by Spiess. For the other Périgordian level at the Abri Pataud, Level 5, the talus deposits are extremely rich in faunal refuse. Unfortunately, because the talus deposits from the Level 3: Lens 2 occupation were destroyed long ago, no direct means exist for adding their faunal sample to that from under the shelter. If, however, the ratio of shelter-to-talus faunal refuse for the Périgordian VI occupations was similar to that for the Périgordian IV (Level 5) occupations, information given by Bouchud (1966, p. 169; 1975, p. 107) suggests that the areal density of talus fauna would have equalled or somewhat exceeded that in the shelter proper. Furthermore, to the 71.5 kg of Level 3: Lens 2 fauna studied by Spiess (1979, p. 206) must be added the faunal refuse from the southern "passageway" connecting the "long-house" habitation area with the mouth of the shelter. (The fauna from the "passageway" was not studied because of the lack of stratigraphic differentiation in that area.)

In summary, then, no very close estimates can be made of group size or duration of occupation for the Périgordian VI at the Abri Pataud. There were at least six occupational

episodes, and even where the data are best—for the occupations of Lens 2—recovery of both artifactual material and faunal refuse from those occupations was far from complete.

Information on the age of the Périgordian VI occupations at the Abri Pataud is provided by both chronometric and relative dating techniques. Four radiocarbon dates have been obtained from Level 3 samples, two of burnt bone

GrN-1864: 18,470 B.P. ± 280
(Vogel and Waterbolk 1963, p. 166)
GrN-1892: 21,540 B.P. ± 160
(ibid.)

and two of unburnt bone

GrN-4506: 22,780 B.P. ± 140
(Vogel and Waterbolk 1967, p. 114)
GrN-4721: 23,010 B.P. ± 170
(ibid.)

The sample for GrN-4721 is from Lens 2; provenience information for the other three samples is not published, but it is most likely that they too came from Lens 2. For reasons explained more fully elsewhere (Waterbolk 1971, p. 29), the oldest date is to be regarded as the most nearly accurate, and the time span between the beginning of the Level 3: Lens 2 occupation and the subsequent Level 2 (Proto-Magdalenian) occupation is approximately 1,000 years—between 23,000 and 22,000 B.P. Neither the earliest nor the latest Périgordian VI occupation at the Abri Pataud is dated by radiocarbon.

The relative, geochronological dating of the Périgordian VI at Pataud is based primarily on Farrand's sedimentological work, as discussed above. Although its placement within the Würm III stadial is well understood in general terms, it has not been possible, using the paleoenvironmental data now available, to arrive at a completely satisfactory correlation between the Périgordian VI occupations at the Abri Pataud and those at the nearby site of Laugerie-Haute. Based on his study of the sediments of Laugerie-Haute, Laville (1975, pp. 378, 379, tableau 5, p. 383) has suggested a correlation that would make all the Périgordian VI occupations at Pataud (assigned to his Périgord VIIb climatic phase of the Würm III) earlier than any of those at Laugerie-Haute (assigned to his phases VIIc and VIII); this is a suggestion by no means discordant with the comparative artifact-typological data (Clay 1968). The major issue here is the geochronological placement of the weathering episode responsible for the development of a soil in Eboulis 2-3: Light Reddish Brown. Stating that the mild climatic interval in question is simply not recorded in the Laugerie-Haute sedimentary sequence, Farrand (1975, p. 64) questions Laville's correlation of the Pataud soil development. It seems likely that only the addition of evidence of a different sort—for example, a more informative palynological sequence

Table 1

DISTRIBUTION OF THE TABULATED ASSEMBLAGE FROM LEVEL 3

Artifact Category	n
Flint Tools Shown on Cumulative Graph	1,309
Miscellaneous Slightly Retouched and/or Utilized Blades	54
Miscellaneous Slightly Retouched and/or Utilized Flakes	88
Broken Burins (too fragmentary to classify)	13
Nuclei, Slightly Worked Nodules, and Flint Chunks	397
Artifacts of Stone Other than Flint	53
Perforated Shells	5
Artifacts of Tooth, Bone, Antler and Ivory	148
Total Tabulated Assemblage	2,067

from the Abri Pataud—could resolve this correlational problem.

THE ARTIFACT INVENTORY

The Level 3 assemblage consists of 2,067 tabulated artifacts (table 1), plus untabulated quantities of art objects (discussed separately; see p. 104), river-stones brought into the site mainly for use in cooking, and *débitage* flakes resulting from the production of flint tools.

The contents of most of the flint industry are summarized in table 2, which employs the 92-type list established for the French Upper Palaeolithic by de Sonneville-Bordes and Perrot (1954–1956). The distribution given in table 2 is shown also in a graph of cumulative percentage frequency (fig. 1) drawn in the standard format (de Sonneville-Bordes 1954). For purposes of comparison, figure 1 shows also the cumulative graph for the later units (REAR plus FRONT:UPPER) of Level 5, Périgordian IV. Various typological indices based on the type frequencies (ibid.) are also given.

The presentation of the flint industry in terms of table 1 and figure 1, along with the discussion of these data appearing below, will serve to introduce the Level 3 assemblage in terms that are comparable wth a larger body of published material on French Upper Palaeolithic sites. The major tool classes—i.e., scrapers, burins, backed tools, truncated pieces, and pieces with marginal retouch—are subjected to further analysis in the following chapters. It is these chapters that constitute the major part of this study; comment concerning these tool classes as they appear on the cumulative graph will be brief, and references to illustrations of these tools are omitted from the present chapter. Some tools—e.g., perforators, notched pieces—are not subjected to attribute analysis; they are discussed only in this chapter, and illustration references to them are included here.

It is important to note that tabulation of the flint industry in terms of the de Sonneville-Bordes and Perrot typology and the attribute analysis presented in the following chapters are two different operations with quite different requirements. Insofar as is possible, the 92-type list includes all flint tools,

complete or broken, in good condition or damaged. Tools that are too fragmentary or badly damaged, however, must be excluded from the attribute analysis. Also, tools that fit the definition of a single type in a typology designed for maximum comparability and wide application may be divided into several different typological entities within the context of a single given assemblage. The reverse case also occurs; in some cases the standard typology splits into two or more types a category that in the specific context is a single typological entity. For these reasons, then, the total frequencies and the distributional details of the cumulative graph are not exactly the same as those of the attribute analysis. The two ways of presenting the flint industry are different, and each should be considered in its own terms. Separately they are internally consistent, but the bodies of information given by the two are not exactly comparable.

ATTRIBUTE TERMINOLOGY AND OTHER CONVENTIONS

Because much of this report deals with the variation in stone-tool attributes, several explanatory remarks are in order. Unless otherwise indicated, the attribute systems here used to describe the lithic artifacts are those explained in detail in Movius et al. (1968). It was the wish of the Abri Pataud project director, Hallam L. Movius, Jr., to include in this report as large a sample as possible of the attribute data on which the study is based. After having experimented with several different techniques of presentation, Movius decided to present many of the attribute data for the illustrated examples of the major classes of flint tools in the form of detailed figure captions. The original suite of illustrated artifacts was supplemented with newly drawn examples in order to have a representative array of attribute variation in the Périgordian VI. Although the data in the captions are not, of course, sufficient for reanalysis by other workers, they do, we believe, offer a clear understanding of the way the attribute systems were used in practice. For chipped stone tools, the terms "proximal" and "distal" have their normal meanings when they appear in the captions—the end containing the platform and bulb and the opposite end, respectively, both in the bulbar axis. Sometimes, however, an illustrated artifact is not drawn in a bulbar axis orientation, or the proximal/distal determination could not be made with certainty. In these cases, the terms "top" and "bottom" are used in the captions, referring solely to the orientation of the drawing. For artifacts of bone, antler, or ivory, "proximal" refers to the end of the tool or weapon toward or closer to the instrument of hafting or prehension (what might often be called the base of the tool). "Distal" refers to the opposite end, usually the primary piercing end of weapon armatures and certain pointed tools. The numbers appearing within parentheses immediately following the object numbers in the figure captions to the artifact illustrations are the original catalogue numbers of the artifacts in question—e.g., the catalogue number of the perforator shown in figure 2, number 17, is

"1852." Finally, the enclosure within parentheses of some percentage values appearing in the attribute distribution tables indicates that they are based on samples of less than 50 objects; percentages of larger samples are shown without parentheses.

DISCUSSION OF THE CUMULATIVE GRAPH

Scrapers

Scrapers in Level 3 are less common (IG = 13.76) than in the later units of Level 5 (IG = 21.80). End-scrapers and atypical end-scrapers are most numerous and of equal frequency. Double and ogival end-scrapers are rare. End-scrapers on retouched blades or flakes are virtually absent (this differs

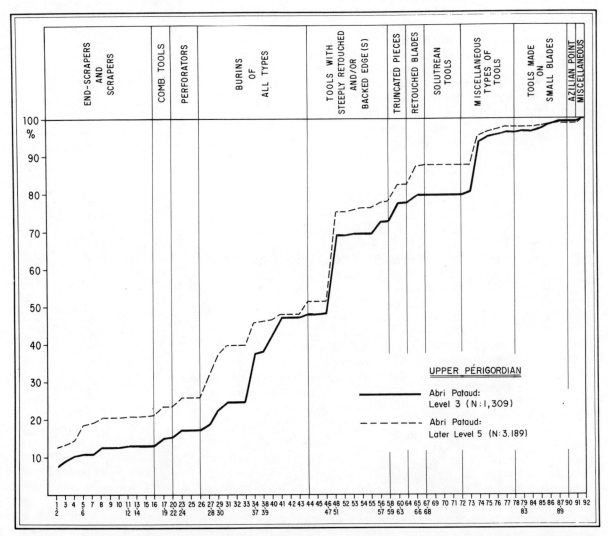

Figure 1. CUMULATIVE GRAPHS FOR THE ASSEMBLAGE SAMPLES FROM LEVEL 3 (SOLID LINE) AND LATER LEVEL 5 (DASHED LINE) AT THE ABRI PATAUD.

Table 2
DISTRIBUTION OF TOOL TYPES AND INDICES OF TOOLS FROM LEVEL 3
SHOWN ON THE CUMULATIVE GRAPH

Type No.	Type	n	%
1	End-Scraper	54	4.13
2	Atypical End-Scraper	54	4.13
3	Double End-Scraper	21	1.60
4	Ogival End-Scraper	15	1.15
5	End-Scraper on Retouched Blade or Flake	8	0.61
6	End-Scraper on Aurignacian Blade	–	–
7	Fan-Shaped End-Scraper	–	–
8	Discoidal Scraper	26	1.99
9	Circular Scraper	–	–
10	Thumbnail Scraper	–	–
11	Carinate Scraper	–	–
12	Atypical Carinate Scraper	2	0.15
13	Thick Nose-Shaped Scraper	–	–
14	Flat Nose-Shaped or Shouldered End-Scraper	–	–
15	Nucleiform Scraper	–	–
16	*Rabot* or Plane	–	–
17	End-Scraper + Burin	23	1.76
18	End-Scraper + Truncated Piece	3	0.23
19	Burin + Truncated Piece	3	0.23
20	Perforator + Truncated Piece	1	0.08
21	Perforator + End-Scraper	–	–
22	Perforator + Burin	2	0.15
23	Perforator	10	0.76
24	*Bec* or Atypical Perforator	13	0.99
25	Multiple Perforator or *Bec*	–	–
26	Micro-Perforator	–	–
27	Symmetrical Dihedral Burin	5	0.38
28	Asymmetrical Dihedral Burin	15	1.15
29	Transverse or Transverse/Oblique Dihedral Burin	5	0.38
30-A	Burin on Broken Surface	47	3.59
30-B	Burin on Unretouched Edge or End of Flake or Blade	11	0.84
31	Multiple Burin Associating Types 27 to 30	13	0.99
32	Busked Burin	–	–
33	Parrot-Beak Burin	–	–
34	Burin on Straight, Right-Angle Truncation	9	0.69
35	Burin on Straight, Oblique Truncation	51	3.90
36	Burin on Concave Truncation	102	7.79
37	Burin on Convex Truncation	13	0.99
38	Transverse Burin on Straight or Convex Lateral Truncation	3	0.23
39	Transverse Burin on Concave Lateral Truncation	5	0.38
40	Multiple Burin Associating Types 34 to 39	65	4.97
41	Mixed Multiple Burin, Types 27–30 + Types 34–39	52	3.97
42	Noailles Burin	2	0.15
43	Nucleiform Burin	–	–
44	Flat-Faced Burin	13	0.99
45	Abri Audi Knife	–	–
46	Châtelperron Point	–	–
47	Atypical Châtelperron Point	–	–

Type No.	Type	n	%
48	Gravette Point	74	5.65
49	Atypical Gravette Point	11	0.84
50	Les Vachons Point	–	–
51	Micro-Gravette Point	181	13.83
52	Font-Yves Point	–	–
53	Gibbous Backed Piece	1	0.08
54	*Fléchette*	–	–
55	Tanged Point	–	–
56	Périgordian Shouldered Point	–	–
57	Shouldered Piece	45	3.44
58	Completely Backed Blade	3	0.23
59	Partially Backed Blade	2	0.15
60	Piece with Straight, Right-Angle Truncation	4	0.31
61	Piece with Straight, Oblique Truncation	13	0.99
62	Piece with Concave Truncation	39	2.98
63	Piece with Convex Truncation	5	0.38
64	Bitruncated Piece	3	0.23
65	Piece with Continuous Retouch on One Edge	23	1.76
66	Piece with Continuous Retouch on Both Edges	9	0.69
67	Aurignacian Blade	–	–
68	Strangled Blade	–	–
69–72	Solutrean Tools	–	–
73	Pick	1	0.08
74	Notched Piece	175	13.37
75	Denticulate Piece	19	1.45
76	Splintered Piece	1	0.08
77	Side-Scraper	9	0.69
78	*Raclette*	–	–
79–83	Geometric Pieces	–	–
84	Truncated Bladelet	–	–
85	Backed Bladelet	10	0.76
86	Truncated Backed Bladelet	14	1.07
87	Denticulate Backed Bladelet	–	–
88	Denticulate Bladelet	–	–
89	Notched Bladelet	9	0.69
90	Dufour Bladelet	–	–
91	Azilian Point	–	–
92	Other Tools, Not Included in Types 1 to 91	12	0.92
	Totals	1,309	100.02

Indices:

IG	(Scraper Index)	13.76
IB	(Burin Index)	31.39
IBd	(Dihedral Burin Index)	7.33
IBt	(Truncation Burin Index)	18.49
IP	(Perforator Index)	1.75
GP	(Périgordian Characteristic Group Index)	30.94

from the situation in the later Level 5). End-scrapers on Aurignacian blades and fan-shaped end-scrapers, both very rare in later Level 5, are completely absent in Level 3. The scrapers counted here as discoidal scrapers, side-scrapers, and atypical carinate scrapers are discussed below (pp. 25–27) in other terms; pieces described as scrapers on amorphous flakes are particularly characteristic of the Level 3 assemblage, and, more generally, of the Périgordian VI. Neither of the atypical carinate scrapers is a characteristic Aurignacian form.

Combination Tools

In Level 3, as in later Level 5, combination tools of any sort are not numerous. The most frequently occurring combinations are end-scraper + burin (fig. 3, no. 16; fig. 12, nos. 16–18; fig. 16, no. 3), end-scraper + truncated piece, and burin + truncated piece (fig. 13, no. 1; fig. 17, no.1).

Perforators

The small series of perforating tools (IP = 1.75) is approximately equally divided between perforators and *becs*. The series is morphologically diverse, and few of the perforators have long, slender, well-degaged points (fig. 2, no. 17). The majority of the series are made on blades (fig. 2, nos. 14, 16) that are often of large size (fig. 2, no. 12) Microperforators are completely absent. Some examples of both perforators (fig. 2, no. 15) and *becs* (fig. 2, nos. 12, 13) are made on flakes. Perforating tools are slightly more numerous in the later units of Level 5 (IP = 2.51), where both multiple perforators and microperforators are present.

Burins

The burin series of Level 3 (IB = 31.39) is relatively larger than that of later Level 5 (IB = 25.74). Overwhelmingly dominant in the burin series are truncation burins (IBt = 18.49), outnumbering dihedral burins by a factor of more than 2 to 1 (IBd = 7.33). It should be noted that the dihedral burin index, IBd, includes burins described below as break burins and unretouched edge/end burins. Single examples of these two kinds of burins account for 4.43% of all graphed tools; thus, true dihedral burins in the restricted sense are far less frequent than is indicated by the dihedral burin index. The internal composition of the burin series of later Level 5 is quite different; the dihedral burin index (IBd = 13.95) is twice as great as the truncation burin index (IBt = 6.69).

Single dihedral burins are predominantly asymmetrical, as they are in later Level 5. The majority of single truncation burins have concave truncations, with oblique truncations next most frequent. In later Level 5, these frequencies are reversed: oblique truncations dominate. Multiple truncation burins are exceptionally common in Level 3 (5.04% of all graphed tools); they are of only minor quantitative importance in later Level 5. Although transverse truncation burins are not frequent, the transverse burin on concave lateral truncation is a distinctive form in the Level 3 burin series. Some of the truncation burins are small and have small burin edges. Two of these (fig. 12, nos. 14, 15), although they lack a stop-notch, may be called Noailles burins. Flat-faced burins of all kinds are very infrequent (0.99% of all graphed tools), more so than in later Level 5 (3.48% of all graphed tools). Many of the transverse dihedral burins and most of the transverse burins on lateral truncations are made on thick flakes; they constitute a distinct morphological variant that is a characteristic feature of the Level 3 burin series.

Figure 2.   LEVEL 3 RETOUCHED BLADES, NOTCHED BLADE, POINTS, PERFORATORS, AND *BECS*

1   (3): Blade with partial fine retouch on the right side; note opposing notches (obverse on right and inverse on left) near proximal end of piece; distal extremity broken.

2   (1125): Blade (*lame à crête*) with slight fine retouch on the right side and edge chipping resulting from use on the left side.

3   (1203): Blade with partial very fine obverse/inverse retouch on both sides; distal extremity broken.

4   (2446): Blade with partial very fine retouch on the left side

5   (1173): Blade with partial scaled retouch on the right side and partial fine retouch on the left side; distal extremity broken.

6   (2525): Blade with broad opposing notches; distal extremity broken.

7   (69): Blade with partial scaled retouch on the right side.

8   (428): Median point on blade; note flat removals on ventral surface at distal extremity.

9   (770): Median point on blade; proximal extremity broken.

10   (1692): Median point on blade; note flat removals on ventral surface on left side of distal extremity.

11   (1147): Slightly asymmetrical point on blade.

12   (86): Coarse *bec* on cortical trimming flake.

13   (888): *Bec* on irregular flake.

14   (425): Asymmetrical perforator on blade; proximal extremity broken.

15   (1488): Coarse perforator on irregular flake.

16   (1290): Asymmetrical perforator on proximal extremity of blade.

17   (1852): Well-made perforator on blade; proximal extremity broken.

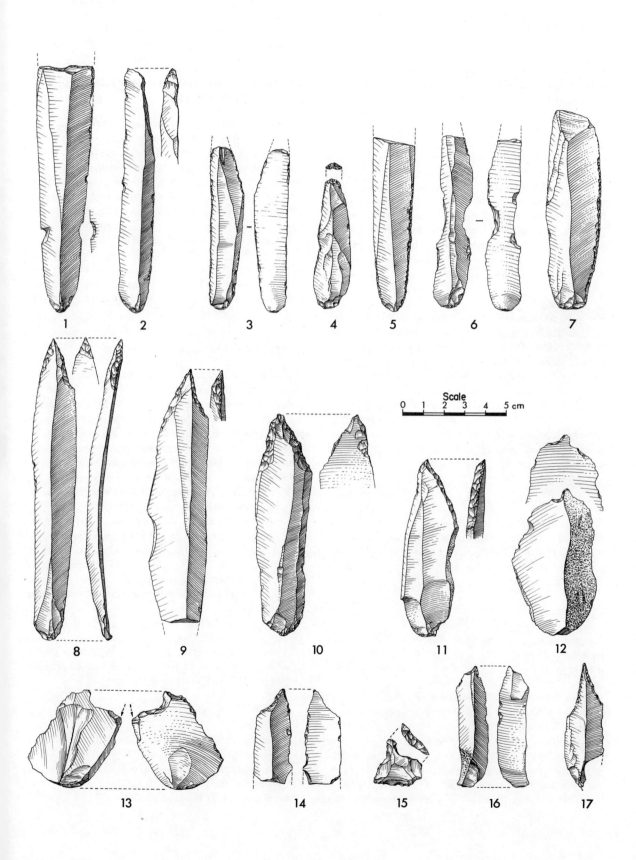

Scale
0 1 2 3 4 5 cm

1   2   3   4   5   6   7

8   9   10   11   12

13   14   15   16   17

Backed Tools

There are no Châtelperron points in Level 3. Gravette and atypical Gravette points (the two categories comprise 6.49% of all graphed tools) and Micro-Gravette points (13.83% of all graphed tools) make up the majority of the backed tool series. The dominance of Micro-Gravette over Gravette points in Level 3 differs from their proportions in later Level 5, where the reverse is true. If the two categories—Gravette and Micro-Gravette points—are combined, however, in Level 3 the combined group's proportion (20.32% of all graphed tools) is comparable to its proportion in Level 5 (22.97% of all graphed tools). *Fléchettes* and Périgordian shouldered points, very rare in later Level 5, are absent in Level 3. Font-Robert points are absent in both levels. The other backed tools—including shouldered pieces, backed blades, backed bladelets, and backed and truncated bladelets—are much less frequent than the combined group of Gravette and Micro-Gravette points; these other backed tools are discussed below (see pp. 39–45) in different terms.

Truncated Pieces

The series of truncated pieces from Level 3 is not large (4.89% of all graphed tools), and bitruncated pieces are virtually absent (0.23%). The overall frequency is about the same as for later Level 5 (4.42% of all graphed tools). Pieces with concave truncation are relatively most numerous in both levels. There are no truncated bladelets in Level 3.

The Périgordian Characteristic Group Index (GP), including all backed tools and truncated pieces, is very high. The value of 30.94, almost one-third of the total graphed tools, is almost exactly the same as the index value of 31.17 for the later units of Level 5.

Marginally Retouched Pieces

Pieces with marginal retouch are very infrequent in Level 3 (2.45% of all graphed tools); they are less frequent there than in later Level 5 (5.14% of all graphed tools). Marginal retouch, which is normally characterized by fine removals, is usually on one edge only.

Various

The one pick is a double-ended tool; both ends have the typical trihedral point. The large series of notched and denticulate pieces (fig. 2, no. 6) calls for no special comment. Splintered pieces are virtually absent.

Three different kinds of tools are included in Type 92 (Miscellaneous). There are five retouched points on large slender blades. The point, formed by heavy, semiabrupt retouch may be either median (fig. 2, no. 9) or asymmetrical (fig. 2, no. 11). Two of the examples have flat, inverse removals on the ventral surface at the point (fig. 2, nos. 8, 10). Five small pieces made on bladelets are considered to be "*pendeloques*" (fig. 27, nos. 1–3). Opposing notches at the proximal end presumably served for suspension. Finally, there are two chopping tools (fig. 25, no. 1) made on globular nodules of flint, one of which is heavily rolled. On both examples, large removals from both faces intersect to form a sinuous, curving working edge at one end of the piece.

ARTIFACTS NOT SHOWN ON THE CUMULATIVE GRAPH

The miscellaneous slightly retouched and/or utilized blades or flakes are pieces that have been slightly modified after their detachment from the core but are not retouched enough or in a sufficiently patterned manner to be assigned to one of the recognized tool categories. Some are certainly broken fragments of tools. A small number of the latter are recognizable as broken burins, but they are too fragmentary for the type to be identified.

There are other artifacts listed in table 1 but not shown on the cumulative graph. These include nuclei, slightly worked nodules, flint chunks, artifacts of stone other than flint, perforated shells, and artifacts of tooth, bone, antler, and ivory, and they are all tabulated and discussed in more detail in various sections below.

SUMMARY AND CONCLUSIONS

The majority of the tabulated assemblage from Level 3 is shown on the cumulative graph. The rest is composed predominately of nuclei, miscellaneous slightly worked flint pieces, and artifacts of various organic materials. The large series of artifacts of tooth, bone, antler, and ivory testifies to excellent conditions of preservation; the richness and variety of these objects, discussed in detail in a following section, is an important characteristic of the Level 3 assemblage.

The cumulative graph for Level 3 is characterized in the first instance by the high frequency of backed tools, the great majority of them being Gravette and Micro-Gravette points. There is also a high frequency of burins, which account for almost one-third of all graphed tools and are heavily dominant over scrapers. Within the burin series, truncation burins are more frequent than all other burins combined. Truncated pieces are not frequent; perforators and pieces with marginal retouch are rare.

The graphs for Level 3 and the later units of Level 5 are generally very similar, although the differences were emphasized in the discussion above. The difference between Level 3's graph and later Level 5's graph may be summarized as follows: In Level 3 one finds

fewer end-scrapers
more burins
truncation burins dominant over dihedral burins, the reverse of the situation in Level 5
Micro-Gravette points dominant over Gravette points, the reverse of the situation in Level 5
fewer pieces with marginal retouch

The general similarity in the two graphs is primarily a result of the high Périgordian Characteristic Group Index, specifically the high frequencies of Gravette and Micro-Gravette points. In both levels, burins are more numerous than scrapers, and combination tools, perforators, and marginally retouched pieces are infrequent. Both graphs have typically Upper Périgordian configurations, and both lack any significant numbers of the three "index fossils"—Font-Robert points, *éléments tronqués* and Noailles burins—of the "Périgordian V" as it is classically understood. Detailed statements of similarity and difference between the Périgordian IV of later Level 5 and the Périgordian VI of Level 3 will be presented in the following chapters; these statements will be made on the basis of the attribute analysis.

Attribute Analysis of End-Scrapers from Level 3

There are 195 studied end-scrapers from Level 3 at the Abri Pataud (figs. 3, 4). Their analysis in this chapter has two goals: (1) to describe them and (2) to compare them with the end-scrapers from Level 5 (Périgordian IV). This pattern of simultaneous description and comparison will be followed in all the analysis sections that follow.

SCRAPING EDGE CONTOUR

The most frequent scraping edge contour (see table 3) is arc-of-circle (fig. 3, no. 4; fig. 4, no. 2), which occurs on one-third of the end-scrapers in the sample. Frequencies of asymmetrical (fig. 3, nos. 6, 13) and irregular (fig. 3, no. 9;

Figure 3. LEVEL 3 END-SCRAPERS AND COMBINATION TOOL

SHAPE OF END

Arc of Circle		Blunt Point		Asymmetrical		Flattened		Irregular	
1	(1): Double; 140°; 1.50 cm; both extremities	15	(19)	2	(820)	7	(382)	5	(305)
		16	(2032): Top	3	(752): Bottom; not included in studied sample			9	(1113)
4	(620): 120°; 1.25 cm			6	(148)			10	(1884): Top
8	(1724): 150°; 1.25 cm			10	(1884): Bottom			12	(1705)
11	(1839): 100°; 1.50 cm			13	(820)			14	(16)
				17	(1885): Bottom			17	(1885): Top

RETOUCH ANGLE

Acute		Medium		Steep		Perpendicular	
4	(620)	1	(1): Bottom	5	(305)	1	(1): Top
11	(1839)	2	(860)	14	(16)	7	(382)
13	(820)	6	(148)	17	(1885): Top		
		8	(1724)	3	(752)		
		9	(1113)	10	(1884): Both extremities		
		12	(1705)				
		15	(19)				
		16	(2032): Top				
		17	(1885): Bottom				

RETOUCH PATTERN

Semi-convergent		Non-convergent	
1	(1): Both extremities	3	(752)
2	(860)	4	(620)
6	(148)	5	(305)
8	(1724)	7	(382)
9	(1113)	10	(1884): Both extremities
15	(19)	11	(1839)
16	(2032): Top	12	(1705)
17	(1885): Bottom	13	(820)
		14	(16)
		17	(1885): Top

MISCELLANEOUS

10 (1884): Continuous fine marginal retouch; left side
16 (2032): Combination tool (retouched truncation burin at bottom)

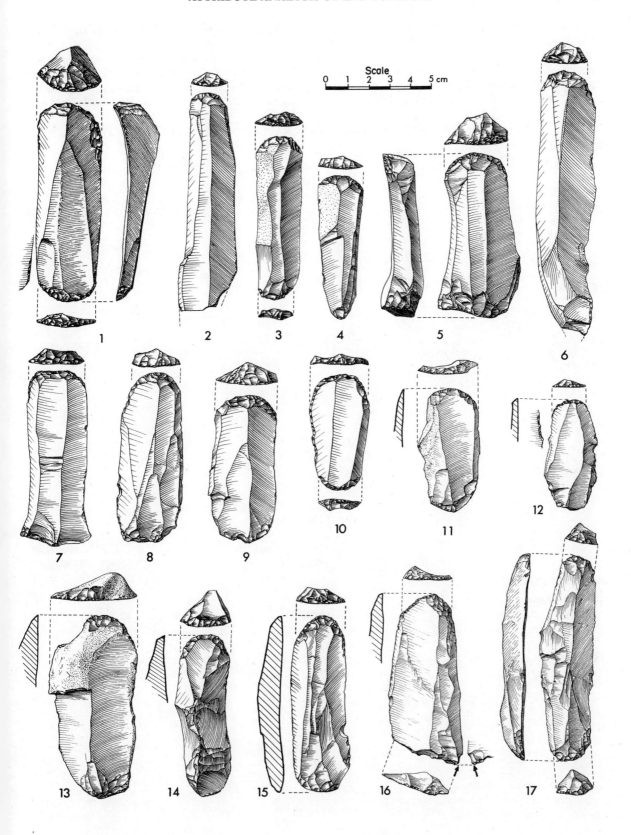

Scale
0 1 2 3 4 5 cm

fig. 4, no. 9) contours are nearly identical, about one-quarter of the sample. Blunt point (fig. 3, no. 15; fig. 4, no. 7) and flattened (fig. 3, no. 7; fig. 4, nos. 4, 8) contours are of minor quantitative importance, each less than 10% of the sample. This distribution of contours is very similar to those of the REAR units of Level 5, especially REAR:UPPER.

RADIUS OF CIRCLE AND DEGREES OF ARC

The distributions of radius of circle and degrees of arc are shown in figure 5. The distributional mode for the radius occurs in the 1.50 cm and 1.25 cm classes, and the generalized arc mode is medium (105°–134°). The Level 3

Figure 4.   LEVEL 3 END-SCRAPERS (Nos. 1–10) AND SCRAPERS ON AMORPHOUS FLAKES (Nos. 11–17)

SHAPE OF END

Arc of Circle	Blunt Point	Asymmetrical	Flattened	Irregular
1 (633): 140°; 2.25 cm	7 (726)	13 (713): Right	4 (723)	9 (542)
2 (807): 130°; 1.75 cm	16 (1972): Left	17 (543): Bottom right	5 (1925)	15 (213)
3 (3715): 150°; 2.00 cm	17 (543): Top		8 (547)	16 (1972): Right
6 (785): 110°; 2.25 cm				
10 (626): 110°; 2.00 cm				
11 (5005): 140°; 2.25 cm				
12 (998): 90°; 2.00 cm				
13 (713): Left: 100°; 2.25 cm				
14 (3998): 100°; 2.00 cm				

RETOUCH ANGLE

Acute	Medium	Steep
2 (807)	4 (723)	1 (633)
12 (998)	5 (1925)	3 (3715)
	6 (785)	8 (547)
	7 (726)	9 (542)
	10 (626)	14 (3998)
	11 (5005)	15 (213)
	13 (713): Right and left	16 (1972): Left
	16 (1972): Right	17 (543): Both

RETOUCH PATTERN

Semi-convergent	Non-convergent
2 (807)	1 (633)
6 (785)	3 (3715)
9 (542)	4 (723)
16 (1972): Right	5 (1925)
	7 (726)
	8 (547)
	10 (626)
	11 (5005)
	12 (998)
	13 (713): Right and left
	14 (3998)
	15 (213)
	16 (1972): Left
	17 (543): Both

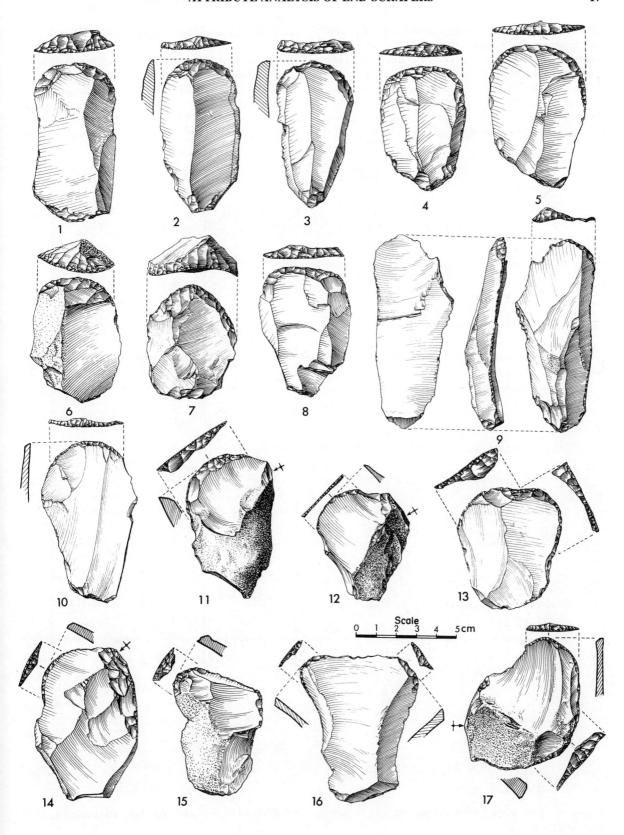

mean values for these attributes are rather different from their counterparts in the later units of Level 5. The mean radius of circle increases through time in Level 5 to achieve maximum values of approximately 1.80 cm. The Level 3 mean of 1.38 çm is considerably smaller. The Level 3 means for degrees of arc (119.85°) is 15° to 20° larger than the mean in any Level 5 unit, indicating that the Level 3 end-scrapers are considerably more rounded than those of Level 5.

RETOUCH ANGLE

The most common retouch angle in Level 3 is medium (see table 4). Pieces with angles duller than medium (fig. 3, no. 5) are more common than those with angles sharper than medium (fig. 3, no. 11). The several attribute frequencies are quite comparable with those throughout Level 5. There is no significant difference, as tested by Chi-square (.75>P>.50),

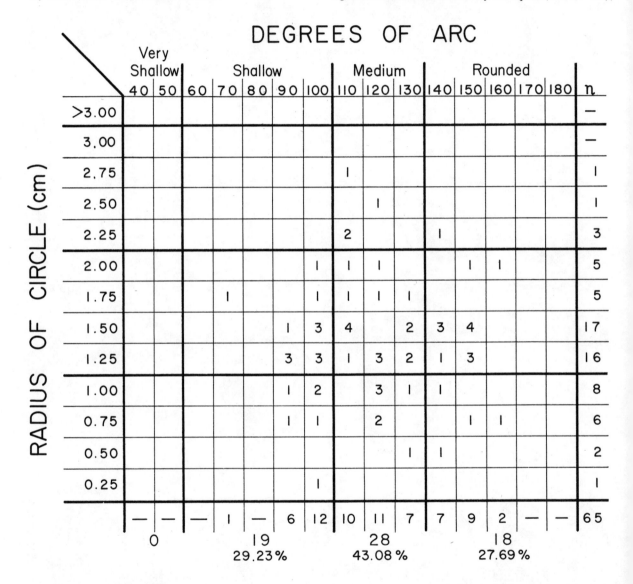

Radius of Circle

$\bar{X} \pm S_{\bar{X}} = 1.38 \pm 0.06 \text{ cm}$

$S = 0.48 \text{ cm}$

Degrees of Arc

$\bar{X} \pm S_{\bar{X}} = 119.85 \pm 2.62°$

$S = 21.10°$

Figure 5. DISTRIBUTIONS OF RADIUS OF CIRCLE AND DEGREES OF ARC OF ARC-OF-CIRCLE END-SCRAPERS IN LEVEL 3.

between the scraping edge angles of arc end-scrapers and of end-scrapers with asymmetrical contour. End-scrapers with irregular contour are, however, significantly duller than arc or asymmetrical pieces (Chi-square test, P<.005).

RETOUCH PATTERN

The distribution of retouch pattern is shown cross-tabulated with that of blank cross-section in table 5. Of the Level 3 end-scrapers, 63.08% have non-convergent retouch, (fig. 3, no. 3; fig. 4, no. 5), 32.82% have semi-convergent retouch (fig. 3, no. 9; fig. 4, no. 2), and only 4.10% have convergent retouch. This distribution is comparable, in broad outline, to those of the later units of Level 5, but convergent retouch is more common in the latter.

ORIENTATION ANGLE AND ASYMMETRY DIRECTION

The combined distributions of orientation angle and asymmetry direction vs. scraping edge contour are shown in tables 6 and 7. For all end-scrapers considered together, an asymmetrical orientation, left or right, is slightly dominant over a symmetrical (90°) orientation. A right asymmetrical orientation (fig. 3, no. 13) is approximately twice as common as a left asymmetrical orientation (fig. 3, no. 15). The proportions of left, 90°, and right orientation in Level 3 are almost exactly the same as those for a pooled sample of all Level 5. Also as in Level 5, the most frequently occurring orientation angle for asymetrically oriented pieces is 80°, with rapidly decreasing frequencies for lower angles.

Table 3

DISTRIBUTION OF SCRAPING EDGE CONTOUR
OF END-SCRAPERS IN LEVEL 3

Contour	n	%
Arc-of-Circle	65	33.33
Asymmetrical	46	23.59
Irregular	48	24.62
Blunt Point	19	9.74
Flattened	17	8.72
Total	195	100.00

Table 4

DISTRIBUTION OF RETOUCH ANGLE
OF END-SCRAPERS IN LEVEL 3

Ret. Angle	n	%
Very Acute + Acute	27	13.85
Medium	92	47.18
Steep	49	25.13
Perpendicular + Overhanging	27	13.85
Total	195	100.01

Table 5

CROSS-TABULATION OF RETOUCH PATTERN AND BLANK CROSS-SECTION
OF END-SCRAPERS IN LEVEL 3

	Triangular	Trapezoidal	Amorphous	Total
Convergent	8	0	0	8 (4.10%)
Semi-convergent	48	12	4	64 (32.82%)
Non-convergent	53	29	41	123 (63.08%)
Total	109	41	45	195
	(55.90%)	(21.03%)	(23.08%)	

Table 6

CROSS-TABULATION OF SCRAPING EDGE CONTOUR *VERSUS* ORIENTATION ANGLE AND ASYMMETRY
DIRECTION OF END-SCRAPERS IN LEVEL 3

	LEFT					RIGHT			
	50°	60°	70°	80°	90°	80°	70°	60°	50°
Arc	1	0	3	7	26	19	7	2	0
Asymmetrical	0	1	5	7	17	8	6	1	1
Irregular	0	0	0	5	24	10	6	3	0
Blunt Point	0	0	0	5	9	5	0	0	0
Flattened	0	0	1	3	11	1	1	0	0
Total	1	1	9	27	87	43	20	6	1

Left = 38 (19.49%)   (44.62%)   Right = 70 (35.90%)

Table 7

CROSS-TABULATION OF SCRAPING EDGE CONTOUR AND ASYMMETRY
DIRECTION OF END-SCRAPERS IN LEVEL 3

		Left	90°	Right	Total
Arc	n	11	26	28	65
	%	16.92	40.00	43.08	100.00
Asymmetrical	n	13	17	16	46
	%	(28.26)	(36.96)	(34.78)	(100.00)
Irregular	n	5	24	19	48
	%	(10.42)	(50.00)	(39.58)	(100.00)
Blunt Point	n	5	9	5	19
	%	(26.32)	(47.37)	(26.32)	(100.01)
Flattened	n	4	11	2	17
	%	(23.53)	(64.71)	(11.76)	(100.00)

Table 8

DISTRIBUTION OF NATURE OF BLANK OF SINGLE
END-SCRAPERS IN LEVEL 3

Nature of Blank	n	%
Blade	67	47.52
Irregular Blade	4	2.87
Trimming Blade	33	23.40
Flake	18	12.77
Trimming Flake	13	9.22
Flake/Blade	6	4.26
Total	141	100.01

When orientation angle and asymmetry direction are investigated separately for each edge contour, the Level 3 end-scrapers are seen to differ from those of Level 5 in one important respect. Throughout Level 5, end-scrapers with asymmetrical scraping edge contour have higher frequencies of right asymmetrical orientation than of symmetrical (90°) orientation. They differ in this way from end-scrapers of other edge contours, for which symmetry is more frequent than right asymmetry. In Level 3 (see table 7), pieces with asymmetrical edge contour do not behave in this fashion. For them, and for arc end-scrapers, frequencies of symmetrical and right asymmetrical orientation are essentially equal. There are no significant differences, as tested by Chi-square, between arc-of-circle and asymmetrical-contour end-scrapers ($.90 > P > .75$), or between these two and irregular-contour pieces, ($.50 > P > .25$) with respect to orientation angle and asymmetry direction.

SCRAPING EDGE WIDTH AND SCRAPING EDGE THICKNESS

The parameters of scraping edge width and thickness for Level 3 end-scrapers are as follows:

Scraping edge width: $\overline{X} \pm s_{\overline{x}} = 26.49 \pm .62$ mm
$s = 8.71$ mm

Scraping edge thickness: $\overline{X} \pm s_{\overline{x}} = 7.48 \pm .22$ mm
$s = 3.02$ mm

The Level 3 mean width is exactly comparable to those for the later units of Level 5; the mean thickness is slightly less than an average figure for later Level 5. Consistent with the latter difference is the fact that the Level 3 value for the thickness/width index (Edge Thickness x 100 / Edge Width) is, at 28.24, lower than the values for later Level 5. This means that the cross-sections of the scraping edges tend to be flatter and less "blocky" in Level 3 than in Level 5.

The relationships among scraping edge width, radius of circle, and degrees of arc for arc end-scrapers are somewhat different for Levels 5 and 3. Throughout Level 5, mean scraping edge width increases gradually, but the mean degrees of arc (roundness) remains essentially constant, causing a gradual increase in the mean radius of circle. Between later Level 5 and Level 3, the mean scraping edge width remains the same, but the mean degrees of arc increases markedly, i.e., the scraping edge becomes more rounded. The effect of this is to diminish the mean radius of circle, even though the absolute width of the edge does not change. The kind of change recorded within Level 5 was interesting in that the morphological standard for an arc-of-circle scraping edge remained remarkably uniform even in the face of changing blank dimensions. With the Level 3 series, on the other hand, it is the morphological standard itself that has changed.

END OF BLANK

The great majority (70.92%) of the 141 single end-scrapers are made at the distal end of the blank, 24.11% are made at the proximal end, and 4.96% are indeterminate. In Level 5, a proximal location becomes more frequent in the later units, but the frequency of Level 3 proximal locations surpasses the Level 5 maximum (20%, in REAR:LOWER).

NATURE OF BLANK

The distribution of nature of blank for single end-scrapers is shown in table 8. The great majority (73.76%) are made on blades, predominantly of the regular, nontrimming variety (fig. 3, nos. 6–9), but the proportion of flakes (fig. 4, nos. 4–8) is relatively high (21.99%), higher than in the later units of Level 5. Chi-square tests show that there are no significant differences in blade-to-flake proportions between arc- and asymmetrical-contour scrapers ($.50 > P > .25$), or between these two and irregular-contour pieces ($.99 > P > .975$).

LENGTH

The mean length of the 87 complete, single end-scrapers is 66.25 ± 1.69 mm, and the standard deviation is 15.73 mm. This mean value is precisely in the range of the later units of Level 5.

BLANK CONTOUR

The distribution of blank contours and their cross-tabulation with scraping edge contours are shown for all single end-scrapers in tables 9 and 10. It is apparent from the former that most of the end-scraper blanks are either irregular (contour 6) (fig. 3, no. 12) or parallel-sided (contour 1) (fig. 4, no. 1). The frequency of irregular blank contour (42.55%) is much higher than in any of the later units of Level 5. The occurrence of rectilinear but nonparallel sides is quite rare, with frequencies generally lower than in later Level 5. Fan-shaped pieces (contour 3) are present in Level 3 in approximately the same low proportion (2.13%) as in later Level 5. The major difference between the two levels is the great increase of nonrectilinear contour in Level 3, reversing a trend toward increasing rectilinear contours in Level 5.

In table 10, end-scrapers with indeterminate contour (contour 7) are excluded, and the remaining pieces are grouped into regular and irregular categories. A Chi-square test (with the blunt point and flattened samples pooled) shows that the frequency differences among scraping edge contours are not significant ($.25 > P > .10$). This situation differs from that in the later units of Level 5, in which irregular scraping edge contour has a significant association with irregular blank contour, as does the arc scraping edge contour with a regular blank contour.

Table 9

DISTRIBUTION OF BLANK CONTOUR OF SINGLE
END-SCRAPERS IN LEVEL 3

Contour	n	%
1	55	39.01
2	7	4.96
3	3	2.13
4	6	4.26
5	1	.71
6	60	42.55
7	9	6.38
Total	141	100.00

Table 10

CROSS-TABULATION OF SCRAPING EDGE CONTOUR AND BLANK CONTOUR OF
SINGLE END-SCRAPERS IN LEVEL 3

		Reg. Contours (1, 2, 3, 4, 5)	Irreg. Contours (6)	Total
Arc	n	23	22	45
	%	(51.11)	(48.89)	(100.00)
Asymmetrical	n	16	12	28
	%	(57.14)	(42.86)	(100.00)
Irregular	n	15	19	34
	%	(44.12)	(55.88)	(100.00)
Blunt Point	n	7	5	12
	%	(58.33)	(41.67)	(100.00)
Flattened	n	11	2	13
	%	(84.62)	(15.38)	(100.00)

BLANK CROSS-SECTION

The distribution of blank cross-section (cross-tabulated with retouch pattern) is shown in table 5. Triangular is the dominant cross-section, present on a majority of pieces (fig. 4, no. 6). Frequencies of trapezoidal (fig. 3, no. 7) and amorphous (fig. 3, no. 13) cross-sections are essentially equal. This distribution is quite different from those of the later units of Level 5, where trapezoidal cross-section has a majority frequency and where amorphous cross-section is of small quantitative importance.

As in Level 5, however, there is in Level 3 a significant association of convergent and semi-convergent retouch pattern with triangular cross-section and of non-convergent retouch pattern with trapezoidal and amorphous cross-sections (Chi-square test, $P < .005$).

MARGINAL RETOUCH

In Level 3, 16 (18.39%) of the 87 complete single end-scrapers and 6 (11.11%) of the 54 broken single end-scrapers bear some kind of marginal retouch. This difference between complete and broken pieces exists also in Level 5, and in neither level is it explicable in terms of retouch localization toward the posterior end of the tool. The Level 3 frequencies of marginal retouch are lower than average frequencies for the several units of later Level 5.

The occurrence of marginal retouch in each marginal zone is shown in table 11, for complete single end-scrapers only. In spite of the small sample, from inspection it is obvious that there is a preference for marginal retouch on the anterior third of the tool but that left-right totals are approximately equal. In later Level 5, there are no preferred marginal retouch loci in terms of thirds or sides of the blank.

Table 12 shows the distribution of kinds of marginal retouch on all single end-scrapers. All types listed are of the normal or obverse variety; inverse marginal retouch, of some quantitative importance in later Level 5, is absent in the Level 3 series. The modal retouch type is "fine," accounting for one-half of the occurrences (fig. 3, no. 10; fig. 4, no. 9). This figure is much higher than in any unit of Level 5. The proportion of heavy retouch is comparable with the later

Table 11

DISTRIBUTION BY ZONES OF MARGINAL
RETOUCH ON COMPLETE SINGLE END-SCRAPERS IN LEVEL 3

Zones	Left	Right	Total
Anterior ⅓	(Zone 1)	(Zone 2)	
	5	9	14
Middle ⅓	(Zone 3)	(Zone 4)	
	2	3	5
Posterior ⅓	(Zone 5)	(Zone 6)	
	3	2	5
Total	10	14	24

Table 12

DISTRIBUTION OF MARGINAL RETOUCH TYPES
ON SINGLE END-SCRAPERS IN LEVEL 3

Retouch Type	n	%
Fine	11	(50.00)
Heavy	6	(27.27)
Scaled	4	(18.18)
Stepped	0	–
Aurignacian	0	–
Other	1	(4.55)
Total	22	(100.00)

Level 5 values. Scaled retouch is much less frequent in Level 3 than in Level 5. Stepped retouch is absent in Level 3. The piece listed as having "other" marginal retouch is a backed blade.

TOOL DISPOSITION ON BLANK

Of the 195 end-scraper scraping edges in the Level 3 series, 32 (16.41%) occur on double end-scrapers (fig. 3, nos. 1, 10, 17), and 22 (11.28%) occur on combination tools (fig. 3, no. 16). The double end-scraper frequency is higher than in any unit of Level 5, but the combination tool frequency is comparable with that for Level 5: REAR:UPPER. There is no tendency for any one of the several scraping edge contours to occur as part of a double scraper or combination tool (Chi-square test, .95>P>.90). Furthermore, the association patterns of scraping edge contours on double end-scrapers follow a random distribution (Chi-square test, .75>P>.50). There is no tendency, as there seems to be in Level 5, for like contours to associate with like.

SUMMARY

End-scrapers in Level 3 are characterized by a high proportion of very regular scraping edges, either arc-of-circle or asymmetrical. The variation between these two contours seems to be continuous, and indeed attribute clusterings that would define natural typological subgroups within the end-scraper class are not found in the Level 3 series. The typological separateness of Level 5 end-scrapers with asymmetrical contours does not show up in Level 3. The modal scraping edge in the Level 3 series has a medium angle and a nonconvergent retouch pattern. The end-scraper blank is predominantly a blade with triangular cross-section, very often with nonrectilinear sides, and usually without marginal retouch. In a relatively high proportion of cases, scraping edges are combined on the same blank to form double end-scrapers.

The end-scraper series of Level 3 resembles that of later Level 5 in several important respects—the relative proportions of the various scraping edge contours are the same, the distribution of retouch pattern is very similar, and the size of the tools is comparable. On the basis of these attributes alone, especially the scraping edge contour, some degree of typological continuity is evident between the two series. The analysis does not, however, reveal any important attributes with respect to which the Level 3 end-scrapers continue time-directional trends operative in Level 5. Several attributes, including some of the most important, do change essentially unidirectionally through the Level 5 sequence, but a knowledge of such trends does not permit a valid "prediction" of the characteristics of the Level 3 series. In two instances—the proportions of regular blank contour and of marginal retouch—the Level 3 frequencies reverse a Level 5 trend.

Some of the principal differences between the two series concern the blank. Thus, in Level 3 the blank is not only less regular; it is also more likely to be a flake. A basic change in either production technique or selection standards is indicated by the predominance in Level 3 of triangular cross-section instead of the trapezoidal cross-section found in Level 5. Also, in Level 3 marginal retouch is less frequent overall, and the distribution of retouch types is different, fine retouch being more frequent and scaled retouch less frequent.

The differences, then, are numerous and real, but their magnitude should not be exaggerated. Many of them have to do with what sort of blank an end-scraper was made upon and not with what sort of end-scraper was made upon a blank. In the latter case, the Level 3 and the Level 5 series are very, very similar, and the differences (e.g., the roundness of arc-of-circle edges) are differences of degree. In general, the attribute analysis confirms the impression received from visual inspection—that the two series are quite similar, representing different stages of what is basically a continuity of technological traditions and habitual modes of tool manufacture within a cultural bloc existing through time. The differences that exist might be understood if we had industries available that were intermediate in time between the Périgordian IV and the Périgordian VI but within the same cultural bloc. It is, indeed, just such industries that the archaeological sequence at the Abri Pataud does not provide.

III

Other Scraper Forms from Level 3

The scraper series of Level 3 consists principally of end-scrapers, but there are small numbers of other scraper forms. These are: scrapers on amorphous flakes, circular scrapers, side-scrapers, end-and-side-scrapers, and miscellaneous steep scrapers. Asymmetrical knives, which may well have been used more as cutting than as scraping tools, are also discussed in this section.

SCRAPERS ON AMORPHOUS FLAKES

The tools described here as "scrapers on amorphous flakes" (fig. 4, nos. 11–17) form a distinct and consistent series characterized by the presence of limited and very often regular scraping edges made, with extremely varied orientations, on irregular and amorphous flakes. The blank is a flake or trimming flake, usually cortical. If the flake is oriented to the bulbar axis, the scraping edge occurs on the left and right sides of the piece with about equal frequencies, more often toward the distal than toward the proximal end. Usually the scraping edge occupies a corner or some other projection of the blank, but in some cases, it is located along the margin of the piece.

The series includes a total of 25 pieces, of which 16 are single (fig. 4, nos. 11, 12, 14, and 15), eight bear two scraping edges (fig. 4, nos. 13, 16, 17), and one bears three scraping edges. As the illustrations make clear, the scraping edge, however placed on the blank, is usually clearly delimited and carefully made. In fact, if the scraping edge were placed at the end of a blade or other elongated blank, these scrapers would certainly be included in the end-scraper series. The general impression is one of an end-scraper scraping edge applied to a convenient corner of an amorphous blank.

This general impression was investigated by comparing the attributes of the scraping edge of the scrapers on amorphous flakes with those of end-scrapers. The distribution of scraping edge contour of scrapers on amorphous flakes is as follows:

arc-of-circle	8 (22.86%)
asymmetrical	9 (25.71%)
irregular	12 (34.29%)
blunt point	5 (14.29%)
flattened	1 (2.86%)

The differences between these frequencies and those for end-scrapers are not significant (Chi-square = 2.17; df = 3; .75>P>.50). For the eight arc-of-circle scraping edges, the

mean radius of circle is 1.84 ± .68 cm, and the mean degrees of arc is 117.50 ± 9.95°. Again, these values are not significantly different from those for arc end-scrapers (Student's t tests, .20>P>.10 and .80>P>.70).

The scraping edge angle is predominantly medium (45.71%), but sharper angles are more common than duller ones (31.43% are acute angles, 14.29% are steep angles; and 8.57% of the angles are perpendicular and overhanging). This is significantly different from end-scrapers (Chi-square = 7.68; df = 2; .025>P>.010), where duller angles are dominant over sharper ones. The retouch pattern on all of the scraping edges but one is non-convergent (97.14%); the one exception is semi-convergent. The blank cross-section is overwhelmingly amorphous (80.00%), with low frequencies of triangular (11.43%) and trapezoidal (8.57%) cross-section.

Scraping edge width and thickness of the scrapers on amorphous flakes are as follows:

Scraping Edge Width: $\quad \overline{X} \pm s_{\overline{x}} = 29.29 \pm 1.10$ mm
$$s = 6.49 \text{ mm}$$

Scraping Edge Thickness: $\overline{X} \pm s_{\overline{x}} = 6.43 \pm .52$ mm
$$s = 3.06 \text{ mm}$$

Compared with the corresponding values for end-scrapers, the width is slightly greater and the thickness is slightly less. The differences fall just short of the .05 significance level (Student's t tests, .10>P>.05 in both cases).

The general impression—that of an end-scraper scraping edge applied to an irregular and amorphous blank—is thus confirmed by this brief analysis. Most of the ways in which scrapers on amorphous flakes differ from end-scrapers follow automatically from the properties of the blank employed. Because the scraping edge is made on the edge rather than across the midline of the blank, the removals are short, and the mean scraping edge thickness is slightly less than the mean scraping edge thickness of end-scrapers. Because the scraping edge is applied to the edge of an often cortical blank, the cross-section is dominantly amorphous. Because clear dorsal ridge patterns are generally absent and because the removals are usually short, the retouch pattern is almost exclusively non-convergent. The location of the edges on the thinner sides of the blank is probably partly responsible for the sharper angle.

In attributes less dependent on the characteristics of the blank, the scrapers on amorphous flakes do not differ significantly from end-scrapers. The distribution of scraping edge

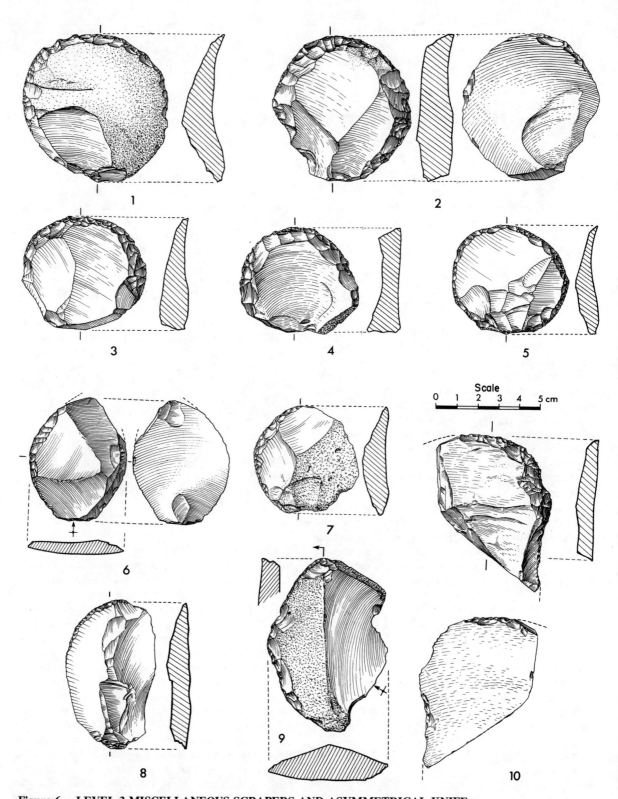

Figure 6. LEVEL 3 MISCELLANEOUS SCRAPERS AND ASYMMETRICAL KNIFE

1 (285): Circular scraper. 2 (1907): Circular scraper. 3 (850): Circular scraper. 4 (66): Circular scraper. 5 (1535): Circular scraper. 6 (1864): Side-scraper. 7 (121): Side-scraper. 8 (9972): Asymmetrical knife. 9 (2952): Side-scraper. 10 (1789): End-and-side-scraper; note inverse retouch.

contour and, in even more detail, the morphological characteristics of the arc-of-circle edge are essentially identical. Thus, although the scrapers on amorphous flakes are *not* end-scrapers, they do seem to represent an "extension" of the technological modes of end-scrapers to a different kind of blank. It is important to note that such pieces are totally absent from the Level 5 scraper series. Their presence in Level 3 represents a clear difference between the Périgordian IV and Périgordian VI assemblages.

CIRCULAR SCRAPERS

There are 13 circular (or subcircular) scrapers in Level 3 (fig. 6, nos. 1–5). They are scrapers on large, generally thick flakes or trimming flakes; the scraping retouch of these scrapers extends around the whole circumference except for the area of the striking platform or any areas of heavy cortex. The striking platform is present, unmodified and unthinned, on all examples. On six of the tools, cortex covers at least half of the dorsal surface. The contour of the piece ranges from circular to irregularly subcircular; the illustrated scrapers are the most regular of the series.

The circular scrapers of Level 3 resemble superficially the *coupoirs* of Level 5, but in fact the two series differ in important ways. The circular scrapers completely lack the patterned *coupoir* complex of point and/or notch and/or inverse removals, and it is not possible to define a standard orientation for them, as is possible for *coupoirs*. The circular scrapers have a curvature of the scraping edge generally not as regular as that of *coupoirs*, although some, especially those in figure 4, numbers 3 and 5, do have the very regular coupoir outline. The circular scrapers are made on thicker blanks than the Level 5 *coupoirs,* and the working edge is much thicker, in terms of both the maximum and minimum measurements. The working edge angle is, on the average,

duller for circular scrapers than for *coupoirs*. Whatever the functional relationship may be between circular scrapers and *coupoirs,* the two kinds of tools are typologically distinct. At the Abri Pataud, the specialized *coupoir* form of the Périgordian IV does not exist in the Périgordian VI assemblage.

SIDE-SCRAPERS AND END-AND-SIDE-SCRAPERS

There are five side-scrapers (*racloirs simples*) in Level 3 (fig. 6, nos. 6, 7, 9), most of which are made on cortical flakes. The scraping edge is in all cases a broad, convex curve. Very similar to these pieces are four end-and-side-scrapers on large flakes (fig. 6, no. 10), on which the side-scraper retouch continues around one end of the blank.

MISCELLANEOUS STEEP SCRAPERS

The rest of the Level 3 scraper series is composed of three miscellaneous steep scrapers on thick, irregular flakes.

ASYMMETRICAL KNIVES

There are two asymmetrical knives in Level 3. One (fig. 6, no. 8) is an absolutely typical example, with the acute working edge on the left side and with the characteristic obverse and inverse removals associated with the right distal corner. The other piece, on a trimming blade, is "atypical" in that the working edge is on the right; the left distal corner is very slightly modified by obverse removals. Both pieces have their equivalents in the Level 5 series, and there is no doubt whatsoever that this specialized and distinctive tool form, appearing for the first time in the Périgordian IV, is present also in the Périgordian VI.

IV

Attribute Analysis of Backed Tools from Level 3

The backed tool series from Level 3 includes two distinct kinds of finished tools—Gravette points and *lamelles à dos tronquées* (literally, "truncated backed bladelets"). The Gravette points are in the overwhelming majority (159 complete or fragmentary tools, excluding segments), whereas the *lamelles à dos tronquées* are numerically insignificant (14 complete or fragmentary tools). In addition to these finished tool-elements, there are several kinds of partially or irregularly backed pieces that probably represent unfinished tools or tools broken in manufacture and/or deliberate byproducts of tool manufacture.

The series also includes 107 backed segments with a broken surface at each extremity; these could be medial portions of broken Gravette points, or they could be *lamelles à dos* (literally, "backed bladelets"). Typological separation must be based on samples as wholes rather than on individual pieces and must proceed within the context of the particular backed tool series of a given assemblage rather than within the strictures of any arbitrary or generally applicable criteria. The analysis of the backed tools of Level 5 suggested that an increase in the relative number of segments is an automatic result of increasing length, *even* if Gravette points are the only kind of backed tool being made. The later units of Level 5, which do not contain a significant *lamelle à dos* series, have butt:segment ratios comparable to those of Level 3, although the Level 5 Gravettes are markedly longer than those of Level 3. This difference in length could indicate that some of the Level 3 backed segments are really *lamelles à dos*.

The possible existence of *lamelles à dos* is relevant also because of the presence in Level 3 of *lamelles à dos tronquées*. Although rare and sporadic examples occur, no unit of Level 5 contains a consistent series of *lamelles á dos tronquées*. The appearance of such a series, albeit small, is an important difference between the Périgordian IV and Périgordian VI assemblages at the Abri Pataud. It is well known from the study of the backed tools of Level 2 (Proto-Magdalenian), where Gravette points are completely absent, that a given number of *lamelles à dos tronquées* can occur in the same assemblage with even larger numbers of backed segments broken at both extremities. These Proto-Magdalenian pieces are made by what has been called the "segmented backed bladelet technique" (Clay 1968; Movius et al. 1968, pp. 49–53; Movius 1968), and it is not suggested at this time that this technique may have been present in Level 3. Rather, the point is simply that the mere existence of *lamelles à dos tronquées* obliges the analyst to consider the

possibility that backed segments may be something other than medial portions of broken Gravette points.

The attributes of the Level 3 backed segments were compared with those of the complete and almost complete Gravette points and with those of *lamelles à dos tronquées*. This comparative investigation seemed to show that the backed segment sample is typologically most comparable to Gravette points. The evidence for this conclusion is presented below, following discussion of the attribute analysis of Gravette points (including segments) and *lamelles à dos tronquées*.

ATTRIBUTE ANALYSIS OF GRAVETTE POINTS

Within the Level 3 Gravette point series, there are two distinct subgroups differentiated on the basis of size. The width distribution is slightly bimodal, with the major mode falling at 4 mm and the secondary, minor mode falling at 10 mm. The length distribution or, even more clearly, the length-width scattergram (fig. 7), also demonstrates the separate existence of a group of long, wide Gravettes. (Predicted lengths were obtained for broken pieces by means of a partial regression equation discussed below.) A series of Chi-square tests failed to reveal any significant differences between the small and large subgroups in attributes other than the metrical dimensions—backing typology, backing side, extremity treatment, or nature of the edge opposite backing. In spite of the lack of such differences, the obvious difference in gross size (fig. 8) seems to justify recognition of two different entities. Although the absolute dimensions of the two subgroups (see below) are smaller than those of the subgroups in Level 5, the relative difference between the small and the large Level 3 Gravettes is enough like that between the Level 5 subgroups to justify retention of the subgroup-AB and subgroup-C terminology. To use these designations for the Level 3 subgroups is to accept the interpretation that the same typological (and functional?) entities exist in both the late Périgordian IV and the Périgordian VI but that in the latter the size range of both subgroups has shifted toward the small end of the scale.

Because subgroups AB and C are differentiated only by their dimensions, the following discussion—except the discussion of length, width, and thickness—applies to all Gravettes, without reference to subgroup.

The Gravette point sample includes 29 (10.90%) complete or almost complete tools, 55 (20.68%) points, 107 (40.23%) segments, and 75 (28.20%) butts. The ratio of points to butts, 1:1.36, indicates relatively more points than in any unit of Level 5, where points become more frequent in the later units. The ratio of butts to segments, 1:1.43, is comparable with values for the later units of Level 5.

When all portions are considered together, frequencies of left-backed (44.65%) and right-backed (55.35%) pieces are nearly equal, with right backing slightly dominant. The frequency of left-backed pieces in Level 3 is higher than that in any unit of Level 5. In Level 5, a trend of increase in left backing through time attains a high value of 14% in REAR:UPPER. When the different portions are considered separately, the frequencies of left-backed pieces are not equal. Those for complete and almost complete pieces and butts are very close, but, just as in Level 5, there are somewhat more left-backed points. These differences are not, however, significant at the .05 level when tested by Chi-square (.50>P>.25). As a further check on the validity of point/butt identification, the combination patterns of both point/butt location and backing side for the fragmentary extremities were compared with those for complete and almost complete pieces. The slight frequency differences are not statistically significant at the designated level (points: P>.24; butts: P>.14). It thus appears that the identification of points and butts is essentially accurate and that the high frequencies of points and of left backing are real characteristics of the Level 3 series.

The distributions of the several attributes of the backing typology are shown in table 13. The majority of Gravette points have heavy backing (86.09%), bidirectional backing (61.28%), and a triangular cross-section (82.71%) (fig. 8, no. 3; fig. 9, nos. 1, 10). Comparison of these figures with those of Level 5 shows that both heavy and bidirectional backing increase in frequency through time to achieve maximum values of 75% and 44% respectively in FRONT:UPPERa. The Level 3 Gravettes thus continue Level 5 trends but carry them further. There is no change in the frequency of triangular cross-section in Level 5, all units having about 70% of this attribute. The conclusion was drawn that in Level 5 the backing technique changes, but the nature of the blank itself remains rather constant. The higher frequency of triangular section in Level 3 suggests a slight shift in patterns of blank production.

Gravettes with partial backing account for 3.58% of the sample; this figure is comparable with those for the later units of Level 5. Only two Gravettes (0.75%) are gibbous (fig. 9, no. 15). An important proportion (7.14%) of Gravettes are made on spalls (presumably mostly burin spalls) rather than on blades or bladelets (fig. 8, no. 9). Similar pieces are present in Level 5 from FRONT:LOWER through REAR, but they are extremely rare (six pieces in the whole level). Thus, the greatly increased use of spalls is certainly one way

in which the Périgordian VI series differs from that of the Périgordian IV.

The edge opposite the backing is most frequently (39.85%) unretouched and unutilized. Modified edges are about equally divided between utilization (32.71%) and retouch (27.44%). Compared with those of Level 5, there are fewer Level 3 Gravettes with retouch, and more that completely lack any modification of the edge. As in Level 5, segments are more often retouched than points or butts. For those Gravettes of Level 3 bearing retouch on the edge opposite backing, the retouch is predominantly partial (53.42%) (fig. 8, nos. 24, 28) and obverse (61.64%). Partial obverse retouch is characteristic of the later units of Level 5, and the Level 3 values are precisely in the range of the later units of Level 5. As in Level 5, obverse-inverse retouch is very infrequent.

The Level 3 Gravettes are characterized by a high frequency (32.35%) of unretouched butts (table 14). Twenty-four of these (23.53%) are of the Unretouched-1 class, i.e., the striking platform of the blank is not present (fig. 9, nos. 7, 12). Unretouched-1 is, in fact, the most frequent butt class in the sample. This frequency of Unretouched-1 butts is higher than that found in any unit of Level 5 (the maximum in Level 5 is 12%, in FRONT:UPPERb), where this attribute does not change regularly through time. The Level 3 frequency of Unretouched-2 butts (striking platform present) is again much higher (n=9; 8.82%) than in all of Level 5 except the two units of REAR (fig. 8, nos. 1, 5). It was shown that in the latter, the frequency of Unretouched-2 butts is associated with the presence of the large subgroup-C Gravettes. There is no such non-random association in Level 3. Thus, the high frequency of unretouched butts in Level 3 forms a distinct difference between the Périgordian IV and the Périgordian VI, and one in which the trends in the former do not foreshadow the situation in the latter.

Of the 69 butts that are formed by retouch, the frequencies of obverse (n=31; 44.93%) (fig. 8, nos. 16, 18) and inverse (n=33; 47.83%) (fig. 8, no. 6) are essentially equal, whereas obverse-inverse retouch is infrequent (n=5; 7.25%). For Level 5, the level as a whole is characterized by predominantly inverse butt treatment. There was, however, a short time, visible in both REAR and FRONT:UPPER, when obverse butt treatment was important or even dominant. The latest Level 5 units show a dominance of inverse butt treatment, however, so it cannot be said that the Level 3 Gravettes simply continue the Level 5 trend in this respect. Obverse-inverse butt treatment is never important in Level 5 (it is always less than 4%), but frequencies do increase slightly through time.

Gravette butts with regular shapes in Level 3 are dominantly asymmetrical (shapes 2 or 3) rather than symmetrical (shape 1), but the latter are more common in Level 3 than in any unit of Level 5. The somewhat greater frequency of shape 3 than shape 2 is the same pattern found throughout

Table 13

DISTRIBUTION OF PRIORITY BACKING TYPOLOGY ATTRIBUTES OF
GRAVETTE POINTS IN LEVEL 3

Type	n		Attribute	n	%
Ia	149		Heavy Backing	229	86.09
Ib	29		Medium Backing	33	12.41
Ic	5		Light Backing	4	1.50
IIa	14			**n**	**%**
IIb	31		Bidirectional Backing	163	61.28
IIc	1		Backing from Ventral	97	36.47
IIIb	33		Backing from Dorsal	6	2.26
IVb	–			**n**	**%**
Vb	4		Triangular Section	220	82.71
VIb	–		Trapezoidal Section	46	17.29
Total	266				

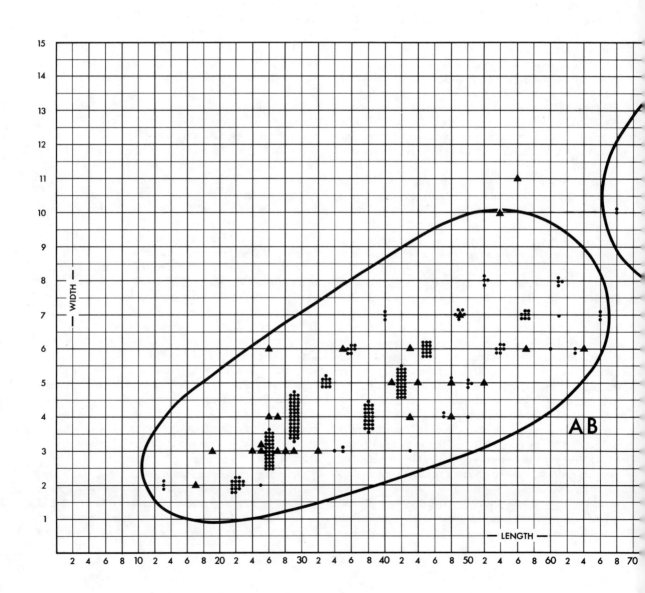

Level 5, where no regular trends of change through time exist. Shape 4 butts (miscellaneous, not assignable to other classes) reach the high frequency of 18.63%, which is comparable to the maximum figure for Level 5 (in REAR:LOWER). As has been mentioned, the occurrence of shape-4 butts can be considered a measure of the descriptive adequacy of the butt typology. Seen in this light, the typology works as well for the Level 3 Gravettes as for the Level 5 Gravettes on which it was developed.

One very important feature of the series of Level 3 Gravettes is the quantitatively important occurrence (21.57%) of Vachons retouch on butts (fig. 8, nos. 14, 15). This is a feature that shows a general increase in time within Level 5, but its maximum frequency (in REAR:UPPER) is only 9%. Not only does the overall frequency of Vachons butt retouch increase in Level 3, but the distributional pattern of butt class changes. Thus, in Level 5, only two (12%) of 17 Vachons butts are of the "classic" obverse-inverse variety; in Level 3,

Table 14
DISTRIBUTION OF THE SEVERAL ATTRIBUTES OF BUTT TYPOLOGY OF GRAVETTE POINTS IN LEVEL 3

Attribute	n	%
Unretouched	33	32.35
Obverse	31	30.39
Inverse	33	32.35
Obverse/Inverse	5	4.90
Shape 1	10	9.80
Shape 2	16	15.69
Shape 3	19	18.63
Shape 4	19	18.63
Shape a	32	31.37
Shape b	3	2.94
Vachons	22	21.57

(% based on n = 102)

five (22.73%) of the 22 Vachons butts are observe-inverse (fig. 9, nos. 4, 6). Although these figures point up an important difference between the Périgordian IV and Périgordian VI Gravettes, they also indicate that the Périgordian VI of the Abri Pataud is certainly not the locus of the maximal occurrence of Gravettes with Vachons retouch.

The point treatment of Level 3 Gravettes is most frequently unretouched (n=27; 36.00% of total sample of 75) (fig. 8, no. 7). As in the case of butts, this value is higher than that found in any unit of Level 5. Of the 48 pieces with retouched point treatment, half (50.00%) have obverse retouch (fig. 8, no. 30), with inverse retouch (39.58%) (fig. 9, no. 3) being more common than obverse-inverse retouch (10.42%) (fig. 8, no. 1). These values are quite comparable with those of Level 5: REAR. Vachons retouch on the point (n=11) attains a frequency in Level 3 of 14.67% (fig. 8, no. 1). This is higher than that found in the later units of Level 5 but comparable with that of FRONT:MIDDLE-1. It was stated earlier that although Vachons retouch on the butt may indeed be of some use as an "index fossil," Vachons retouch at the point does not seem to have the same utility.

The distributions of the metrical dimensions of the Level 3 Gravette points are shown in table 15. Original lengths of fragmentary examples were predicted by the following partial regression equation, based on the relationships present in 29 complete and almost complete pieces:

$$\text{Length} = 3.51 \,(\text{Width}) + 8.77 \,(\text{Thickness}) - 2.32$$

The multiple correlation coefficient is .91, and the standard error of the estimate is 9.38 mm. The mean length (37.45

▲ COMPLETE AND ALMOST COMPLETE

• FRAGMENTARY PORTIONS (Projected Length)

6 8 80 2 4 6 8 90 2 4 6 8 100 2 4 6 8 110

Figure 7. LENGTH-WIDTH SCATTERGRAM OF GRAVETTE POINTS IN LEVEL 3; MEASUREMENTS ARE IN MILLIMETERS.

Figure 8.   LEVEL 3 GRAVETTE POINTS

PORTION STUDIED

Complete	Almost Complete	Point	Segment	Butt
1 (338+384)	3 (851+1799)	9 (572)	20 (1481)	11 (212)
2 (673+1188)	5 (781)	10 (1006)	21 (1703)	14 (49)
4 (281)	13 (1246)	12 (502)	22 (1446)	15 (241)
6 (138+549)		26 (4997)	23 (2102)	16 (863+4969)
7 (1221)		27 (1797)		17 (1798)
8 (1149)		28 (1160)		18 (1771)
24 (1414+1416)		29 (724)		19 (856)
25 (1508)		30 (375)		
		31 (818)		

BACKING SIDE

Left	Right	Indeterminate
4 (281)	1 (338+384)	20 (1481)
8 (1149)	2 (673+1188)	21 (1703)
9 (572)	3 (851+1799)	22 (1446)
13 (1246)	5 (781)	23 (2102)
15 (241)	6 (138+549)	
24 (1414+1416)	7 (1221)	
26 (4997)	10 (1006)	
27 (1797)	11 (212)	
28 (1160)	12 (502)	
29 (724)	14 (49)	
30 (375)	16 (863+4969)	
31 (818)	17 (1798)	
	18 (1771)	
	19 (856)	
	25 (1508)	

NATURE AND EXTENT OF BACKING

Ia	Ib	IIa	IIb	IIIb
2 (673+1188): (Ia+Ib+IIIb)	8 (1149): (Ib+IIIb+Vb)	1 (338+384): (IIa+IIb)	24 (1414+1416)	9 (572)
3 (851+1799): (Ia+Ib)	21 (1703): (Ib+IIIb)	14 (49): (IIa+IIb+IIc)		11 (212)
4 (281): (Ia+ IIb+IVb)	26 (4997): (Partial+Ib+IIIb)	15 (241): (IIa+IIb+IIIb)		12 (502)
5 (781): (Ia+ Ib+Vb)	29 (724): (Ib+IIIb+Vb)	18 (1771): (IIa+IIb)		17 (1798)
6 (138+549): (Ia +Ic+IIa+IIb)		31 (818): (IIa+IIc+IIIb)		25 (1508)
7 (1221)				
10 (1006): (Ia+IIIb)				
13 (1246): (Ia+IIIb)				
16 (863+4969)				
19 (856): (Ia+Ib)				
20 (1481): (Ia+Ib)				
22 (1446)				
23 (2102): (Ia+Ib+Ic)				
27 (1797)				
28 (1160): (Ia+IIIb)				
30 (375): (Ia+IIIb)				

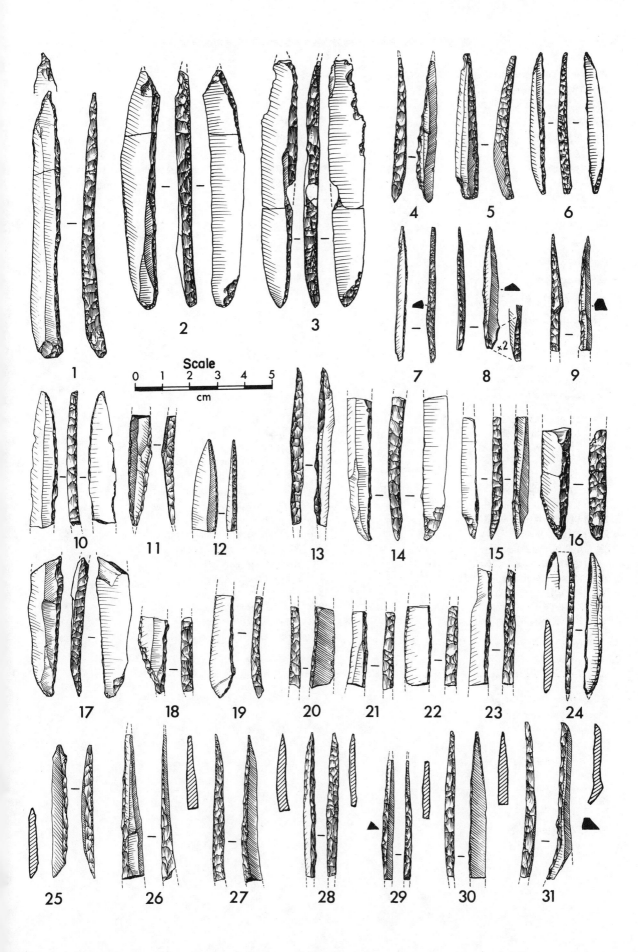

Scale

0 1 2 3 4 5
cm

Figure 8 (continued).

POINT/BUTT LOCATION

Butt Proximal	Butt Distal	Indeterminate
1 (338+384)	4 (281)	16 (863+4969)
2 (673+1188)	9 (572)	18 (1771)
3 (851+1799)	10 (1006)	20 (1481)
5 (781)	12 (502)	21 (1703)
6 (138+549)	13 (1246)	22 (1446)
7 (1221)	15 (241)	23 (2102)
8 (1149)	25 (1508)	28 (1160)
11 (212)	26 (4997)	31 (818)
14 (49)	27 (1797)	
17 (1798)	29 (724)	
19 (856)	30 (375)	
24 (1414+1416)		

POINT/BUTT TYPES

Point

1 (338+384):
Obverse/Inverse-2
2 (673+1188): Inverse-1
4 (281): Unretouched
6 (138+549):
Obverse/Inverse-2
7 (1221): Unretouched
8 (1149): Inverse-1
9 (572): Obverse
10 (1006): Inverse-1
12 (502): Obverse
13 (1246): Obverse/Inverse-1
24 (1414+1416): Inverse-2
25 (1508): Obverse
26 (4997): Unretouched
27 (1797): Inverse-1
28 (1160): Unretouched
29 (724): Unretouched
30 (375): Obverse
31 (818): Unretouched

Butt

1 (338+384):
Unretouched-2
2 (673+1188):
Inverse-4
3 (851+1799):
Inverse-3a;
Vachons
4 (281): Inverse-4
5 (781): Unretouched-2
6 (138+549): Inverse-3a
7 (1221): Inverse-4; Vachons
8 (1149): Obverse-2a
11 (212): Obverse-1
14 (49): Inverse-3a; Vachons
15 (241): Inverse-2a; Vachons
16 (863+4969): Obverse-2a
17 (1798): Inverse-4
18 (1771): Obverse-2a
19 (856): Unretouched-1
24 (1414+1416): Obverse-3a
25 (1508): Unretouched-1

Figure 8 (continued).

EDGE OPPOSITE THE BACKING

Unretouched and Unutilized	Utilized	Retouched (Obverse/Inverse)	Retouched (Obverse)	Retouched (Inverse)
6 (138+549)	1 (338+384)	20 (1481): Continuous	11 (212): Continuous	2 (673+1188): Partial
7 (1221)	3 (851+1799)		16 (863+4969): Partial	28 (1160): Partial
9 (572)	4 (281)		18 (1771): Continuous	
12 (502)	5 (781)		19 (856): Partial	
13 (1246)	8 (1149)		22 (1446): Continuous	
14 (49)	10 (1006)		24 (1414+1416): Partial	
15 (241)	23 (2102)			
17 (1798)	27 (1797)			
21 (1703)	30 (375)			
25 (1508)				
26 (4997)				
29 (724)				
31 (818)				

Table 15

DISTRIBUTION OF LENGTH, WIDTH, AND THICKNESS OF GRAVETTE POINTS IN
LEVEL 3

		Subgroup AB	Subgroup C
Length:	$\bar{X} \pm s_{\bar{X}}$	37.45 ± .70 mm	82.00 ± 3.04 mm
	s	11.23 mm	10.51 mm
Width:	$\bar{X} \pm s_{\bar{X}}$	4.58 ± .10 mm	10.42 ± .42 mm
	s	1.64 mm	1.45 mm
Thickness:	$\bar{X} \pm s_{\bar{X}}$	2.63 ± .05 mm	5.08 ± .42 mm
	s	.83 mm	.79 mm
	n	254	12

Note: Sample values shown are mean ($\bar{X}$), standard error of the mean ($s_{\bar{X}}$), and standard deviation (s).

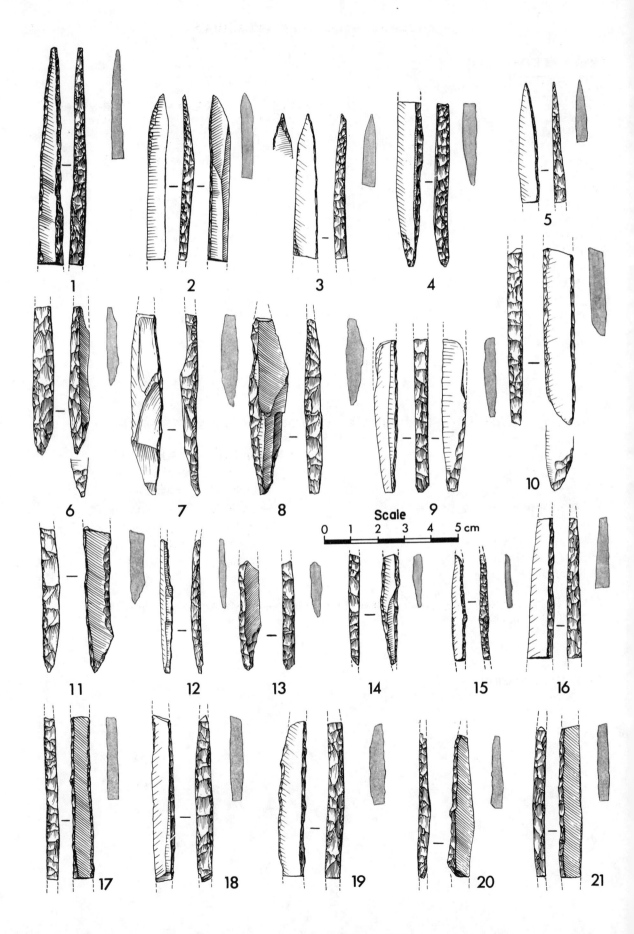

Scale

0 1 2 3 4 5 cm

1   2   3   4   5

6   7   8   9   10

11   12   13   14   15   16

17   18   19   20   21

Figure 9. LEVEL 3 GRAVETTE POINTS

PORTION STUDIED

Almost Complete	Point	Segment	Butt
8 (551)	1 (299+1661)	15 (1145)	4 (1516)
12 (400)	2 (52)	16 (2103)	6 (1022)
	3 (816)	17 (28)	7 (2169)
	5 (1256)	18 (2799)	9 (1769)
		19 (14)	10 (962)
		20 (964)	11 (1695)
		21 (979)	13 (1636)
			14 (1184)

BACKING SIDE

Left	Right	Indeterminate
2 (52)	1 (299+1661)	15 (1145)
5 (1256)	3 (816)	16 (2103)
6 (1022)	4 (1516)	17 (28)
8 (551)	7 (2169)	18 (2799)
11 (1695)	9 (1769)	19 (14)
13 (1636)	10 (962)	20 (964)
	12 (400)	21 (979)
	14 (1184)	

NATURE AND EXTENT OF BACKING

Ia	Ib	IIa
1 (299+1661)	8 (551): (Ib+IIIb)	2 (52): (IIa+IIb)
3 (816): (Ia+Ib)		9 (1769): (IIa+IIb)
4 (1516): (Ia+IIIb)		12 (400): (IIa+IIb+IIc)
5 (1256)		
6 (1022): (Ia+Ib)		
7 (2169): (Ia+Ib)		
10 (962)		
11 (1695): (Ia+Ib)		
13 (1636)		
14 (1184): (Ia+Ib+Ic)		
15 (1145): (Ia+Ic)		
16 (2103)		
17 (28): (Ia+Ib)		
18 (2799): (Ia+Ib+IIb)		
19 (14)		
20 (964): (Ia+Ib+Ic)		
21 (979)		

POINT/BUTT LOCATION

Butt Proximal	Butt Distal	Indeterminate
2 (52)	1 (299+1661)	9 (1769)
6 (1022)	3 (816)	14 (1184)
7 (2169)	4 (1516)	15 (1145)
8 (551)	5 (1256)	16 (2103)
10 (962)	11 (1695)	17 (28)
12 (400)		18 (2799)
13 (1636)		19 (14)
		20 (964)
		21 (979)

Figure 9 (continued).

POINT/BUTT TYPES

Point

1 (299+1661): Obverse/Inverse-1
2 (52): Unretouched
3 (816): Inverse-2
5 (1256): Inverse-1

Butt

4 (1516): Obverse/Inverse; Vachons
6 (1022): Obverse/Inverse; Vachons
7 (2169): Unretouched-1
8 (551): Obverse-3a
9 (1769): Inverse-1; Vachons
10 (962): Inverse-2a; Vachons
11 (1695): Unretouched-1
12 (400): Unretouched-1
13 (1636): Obverse-1
14 (1184): Obverse-1

EDGE OPPOSITE THE BACKING

Unretouched and Unutilized

4 (1516)
6 (1022)
20 (964)

Utilized

5 (1256)
7 (2169)
8 (551)
13 (1636)
15 (1145)
16 (2103)

Retouched (Obverse)

1 (299+1661): Continuous
3 (816): Partial
10 (962): Continuous
11 (1695): Continuous
14 (1184): Continuous
17 (28): Continuous
18 (2799): Partial
19 (14): Continuous

Retouched (Inverse)

2 (52): Partial
9 (1769): Continuous
12 (400): Partial
21 (979): Partial

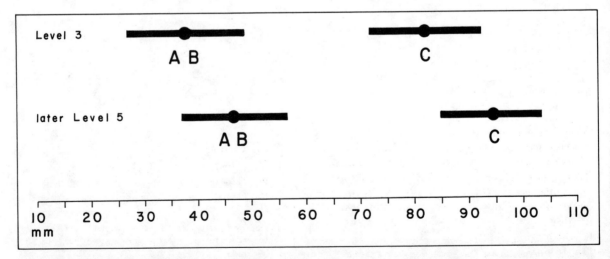

Figure 10. COMPARISON OF LENGTH OF THE GRAVETTE POINTS OF SUBGROUPS AB AND C IN LEVEL 3 AND LATER LEVEL 5. MEAN LENGTH (DOT) AND ONE STANDARD DEVIATION ON EACH SIDE OF THE MEAN ARE SHOWN. LEVEL 3: $\overline{X}_{AB}$ = 37.45 MM, s_{AB} = 11.23 MM, n_{AB} = 254; $\overline{X}_C$ = 82.00 MM, s_C = 10.51 MM, n_C = 12. LATER LEVEL 5: $\overline{X}_{AB}$ = 46.72 MM, s_{AB} = 10.13 MM, n_{AB} = 672; $\overline{X}_C$ = 94.32 MM, s_C = 9.42 MM, n_C = 72.

mm) of the AB subgroup in Level 3 is 4 to 13 mm shorter than the means for the later units of Level 5. That of the C subgroup is 8 to 14 mm shorter than its Level 5 counterparts (see fig. 10). The 45 mm difference between the mean lengths of the Level 3 subgroups is exactly comparable with the differences in the later units of Level 5. It seems quite clear that in terms of the dimensions alone, the same distinction between small and large Gravette points is present both in the late Périgordian IV and in the Périgordian VI. What is striking is the drastic diminution in the absolute size of both kinds of Gravettes in the Périgordian VI.

When all the Level 3 Gravette points are considered together without reference to subgroups, their mean dimensions (length = 39.57 mm; width = 4.85 mm; thickness = 2.74 mm) are, not surprisingly, much lower than the same values for the later units of Level 5. The mean width for Level 3 is, in fact, much lower than that of any Level 5 unit. The width/thickness index (177) and the length/width index (816) for Level 3 are completely outside the ranges of the Level 5 values. This is to say that the Level 3 Gravettes as a series are generally characterized as short, narrow for their thickness, and very "spiky."

The distribution of gross morphology of the 29 complete and almost complete Level 3 Gravettes is as follows: five parallel-sided (fig. 8, no. 25; fig. 9, no. 11), 22 sub-parallel-sided (fig. 8, no. 14; fig. 9, no. 10), one narrow lanceolate, and one asymmetrical lanceolate. The dominance (93.10%) of parallel- and subparallel-sided forms in Level 3 is comparable to all units of Level 5. It is interesting to note the complete absence from the Level 3 series of the Châtelperronoid form. As discussed above, this form in Level 5 was almost exclusively associated with the large subgroup-C Gravettes of the Périgordian IV.

The relationship between the Gravette points of the later units of Level 5 and those of Level 3 can be briefly summarized as follows: There is a large measure of similarity between the two series. They are certainly members of the same tool class, and, moreover, this class seems to have been broken down by the artificers into the same subgroupings. In many details of the attribute constellations, the two series are quite comparable or very similar. The most important difference between them is the smaller size and "spikier" form of the Level 3 Gravettes.[1] Other differences occur in the treatment of the extremities, with the Level 3 pieces having higher frequencies of unretouched butts and points and a higher relative frequency of obverse retouch on butts. Finally, the absence of Châtelperronoid forms in Level 3 represents a clear difference from the Level 5 series. All these different characteristics of the Level 3 Gravettes are ones that could

not be predicted or expected, given a knowledge of the Level 5 trends through time. There are, however, some other features in which Level 3 differs from Level 5 but continues a trend in a direction that was already visible in the latter. Frequencies of left backing and of heavy and bidirectional backing increase through time in Level 5, and the latest Level 5 frequencies are exceeded by those of Level 3. Similarly, the appearance of any significant number of Vachons butts is restricted to later Level 5 units, and the Level 3 frequency for these is considerably higher. This is true not only of all Vachons butt retouch in general but also of the "classic" obverse-inverse Vachons butt retouch in particular.

In several important ways, then, a typological continuity from the Périgordian IV Gravette point series to the Périgordian VI Gravette point series is evident at the Abri Pataud. This typological continuity, present in general as well as in very specific characters, is taken to be a result of cultural continuity, i.e., a continuity in technological traditions and habitual modes of tool manufacture within a cultural bloc continuing through time. Certain it is, however, that recognition of this continuity shown by the Gravette point series must be tempered by a concomitant recognition of important differences between them. Approximately 5,000 years separate the two levels, and the archaeological sequence at the Abri Pataud sheds virtually no light on the typological development that took place in the Gravette point tool class during those years.

ATTRIBUTE ANALYSIS OF *LAMELLES A DOS TRONQUÉES*

The attribute system of *lamelles à dos tronquées* consists of those Gravette point attribute sets that are applicable, plus certain characteristics of the retouched truncations located at the extremities.

The Level 3 series includes only 14 pieces, four of which are truncated or otherwise retouched (see below) at both ends (these are obviously complete tool-elements) (fig. 11, nos. 17, 18) and ten of which have a truncation at one end and an unretouched broken surface at the other (these are possibly, but not certainly, broken tool-elements) (fig. 11, nos. 19–22). If the pieces are oriented with the distal end upwards, five are backed on the left, and nine on the right.

A majority of the pieces have heavy backing (n=9; 64.29%), and backing from the ventral surface only (n=9; 64.29%). Triangular cross-section (n=8; 57.14%) is somewhat dominant over trapezoidal cross-section (n=6; 42.86%). None of the pieces is partially backed, and one is gibbous (fig. 11, no. 18). The edge opposite backing is seldom unmodified (n=1; 7.14%), most often utilized (n=11; 78.57%), and sometimes retouched (n=2; 14.29%). Both retouched examples have partial obverse retouch.

All of the 17 retouched truncations at the extremities are complete, extending across the whole width of the blank. Most of them (n=15; 88.24%) are obverse, i.e., "normal."

---

1. It may be relevant to note that weapon armatures made of organic materials are far more frequent in the Périgordian VI than in the Périgordian IV. A part of the functional range of the large Périgordian IV Gravette points may have been taken over in the Périgordian VI by the various kinds of bone, antler, and ivory sagaies.

The distribution of the angle and shape of the truncations is as follows:

straight–90°	5 (29.41%)
straight–oblique	3 (17.65%)
concave–90°	6 (35.29%)
concave–oblique	3 (17.65%)
Total	17

Obviously, then, a majority of the truncations form a right angle with the working axis of the tool; the shape is about evenly divided between straight and concave.

One of the complete *lamelles à dos tronquées* (fig. 11, no. 23) has a pointed distal end. This point, formed by obverse retouch on the edge opposite the backing, is morphologically equivalent to the anterior extremity of either a Gravette point or the pointed variety of a segmented backed bladelet (17 of which occur in Level 2, Proto-Magdalenian, at the Abri Pataud). The proximal end of the tool bears a concave–90° obversely retouched truncation.

The distributions of the metrical dimensions of *lamelles à dos tronquées* are shown in table 16. Length has a very wide range, from 11 to 52 mm. Pieces with retouch at both extremities fall in the middle of this range; the three shortest

Figure 11. LEVEL 3 GRAVETTE POINTS, *LAMELLES À DOS TRONQUÉES*, AND OTHER BACKED PIECES

GRAVETTE POINTS

1   (2098): Segment, with backing type IIIb; partial obverse retouch on the edge opposite the backing.

2   (398): Segment, with backing type Ia; partial obverse retouch on the edge opposite the backing.

UNFINISHED GRAVETTE POINTS

3   (113): Partial backing of right edge starts from proximal end; no retouch or utilization on edge opposite the backing at butt.

4   (441): Partial backing of left edge starts from proximal end; no retouch or utilization on edge opposite the backing at butt.

5   (1741): Partial backing of right edge starts from proximal end; no retouch or utilization on edge opposite the backing at butt.

6   (686): Partial backing of left edge starts from proximal end. Gravette butt type: Obverse-3a.

7   (1411): Partial backing of left edge starts from distal end; obverse utilization and pseudo-burin removals at point.

9   (687): Partial backing of left edge starts from distal end; no retouch or utilization on edge opposite the backing at point.

10   (1984): Partial backing of left edge starts from distal end; no retouch or utilization on edge opposite the backing at point.

11   (1664): Partial backing of right edge starts at or near distal end (extreme tip missing).

15   (1419): Backed left edge is gibbous; no retouch or utilization on edge opposite the backing at point.

LAMELLE À DOS

16   (318): Backed left edge (Ib+Ic) is gibbous; natural distal extremity is not pointed; no retouch or utilization on edge opposite the backing; broken at proximal end.

LAMELLES À DOS TRONQUÉES (SEGMENTED BACKED BLADELETS) AND PARTIALLY BACKED BYPRODUCTS

8   (1519): Partially backed bladelet on which unpointed natural distal extremity is preserved; broken at proximal end near bulb.

12   (853): Partially backed segment (shouldered bladelet).

13   (1389): Partially backed distal discard (shouldered bladelet).

14   (3171): Partially backed segment (shouldered bladelet).

17   (1604): *Lamelle à dos tronquée.* Complete; backing left; IIIb (IIIb+Vb); utilized edge opposite the backing; complete obverse truncations at both ends.

18   (1875): *Lamelle à dos tronquée.* Complete; backing left; Ia; utilized edge opposite the backing; complete obverse truncations at both ends.

19   (847): *Lamelle à dos tronquée.* Distal extremity; backing right; IIb (IIb+IVb); utilized edge opposite the backing; complete obverse truncation at distal end.

20   (391 + 412): *Lamelle à dos tronquée.* Distal extremity; backing left; Ia (Ia+Ic+IIa); utilized edge opposite the backing; complete obverse truncation at distal end.

21   (346): *Lamelle à dos tronquée.* Proximal extremity; backing right; Ia (Ia+Ib+Ic); utilized edge opposite the backing; complete obverse truncation at proximal end.

22   (360): *Lamelle à dos tronquée.* Distal extremity; backing right; IIIb (IIIb+Vb); utilized edge opposite the backing; complete obverse truncation at distal end.

23   (1236): *Lamelle à dos tronquée.* Complete; backing left; IIIb; utilized edge opposite the backing; point formed by obverse retouch at distal end; complete obverse truncation at proximal end.

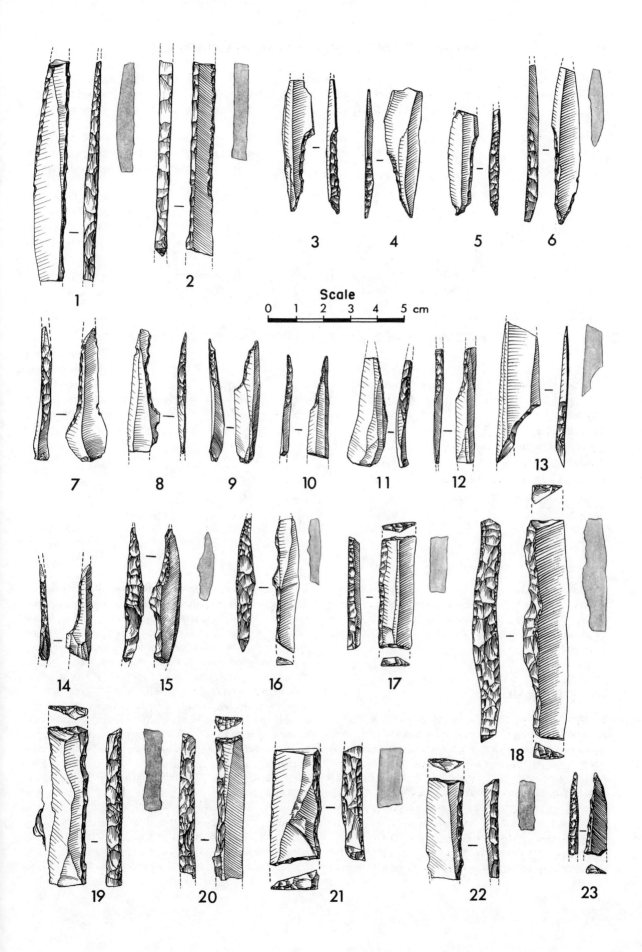

Scale

0 1 2 3 4 5 cm

Table 16

DISTRIBUTION OF LENGTH, WIDTH, AND
THICKNESS OF *LAMELLES À DOS TRONQUÉES* IN
LEVEL 3

Length:	$\bar{X} \pm s_{\bar{X}}$	25.21 ± 2.77 mm
	s	10.35 mm
Width:	$\bar{X} \pm s_{\bar{X}}$	7.42 ± .46 mm
	s	1.73 mm
Thickness:	$\bar{X} \pm s_{\bar{X}}$	3.43 ± .27 mm
	s	1.00 mm
	n	14

Note: Sample values shown are mean ($\bar{X}$), standard error of
the mean ($s_{\bar{X}}$), and standard deviation (s).

Table 17

ATTRIBUTE DISTRIBUTIONS OF SEVERAL KINDS OF BACKED TOOLS IN LEVEL 3

Attribute	Gravettes Comp. and Almost Comp.	Gravettes Segments	Lamelles à Dos Tronquées	Shouldered Bladelets	Shouldered Bladelets and Lamelles à Dos Tronquées
Heavy Backing	(72%)	90%	(64%)	(68%)	(67%)
Bidirectional Backing	(55%)	61%	(36%)	(18%)	(28%)
Triangular Section	(86%)	82%	(57%)	(59%)	(61%)
Retouched Edge Opposite Backing	(28%)	35%	(14%)	–	–
Broken Length $\bar{X}$	–	19.57 mm	25.21 mm	–	–
Width $\bar{X}$	5.62 mm	4.50 mm	7.42 mm	5.64 mm	6.33 mm
Thickness $\bar{X}$	3.17 mm	2.46 mm	3.43 mm	2.86 mm	3.08 mm
$\bar{W} \times 100 / \bar{Th}$	177	183	216	187	206
n	29	107	14	22	36

pieces have a broken surface at one extremity, as does the longest piece. Such a distribution makes it clear that one cannot safely say that all pieces ending in a broken surface are of necessity broken tool-elements. The width/thickness index is 216.

BACKED SEGMENTS

In order to determine whether some or all of the backed segments in the Level 3 series are really *lamelles à dos,* their attributes were compared with those of complete and almost complete Gravette points, on the one hand, and of the *lamelles à dos tronquées*, on the other. The attributes that were employed in the comparison are heavy backing, bidirectional backing, triangular cross-section, retouch on the edge opposite the backing, length (for the segments and *lamelles à dos tronquées* only), width, and thickness (see table 17).

When tested by Chi-square, backed segments do not differ significantly from complete and almost complete Gravettes in frequencies of bidirectional backing, triangular cross-section, or retouch on the edge opposite backing. They do, however, have a significantly higher proportion of heavy backing than the Gravette control sample (Fisher's Exact Test: P = .02) has. Furthermore, the backed segments are significantly narrower and thinner than complete and almost complete Gravettes (Student's t Tests: .02>P>.01 and P < .001 respectively). The width/thickness relationship is, however, quite similar, as shown by the index values (183 for segments; 177 for complete and almost complete Gravettes). Compared with the *lamelles à dos tronquées,* the backed segments differ significantly in having a lower proportion of triangular cross-section (Chi-square = 3.77; df = 1, P = approximately .05) and of retouch on the edge opposite backing (Chi-square = 4.22; df = 1; .05 >P>.025). Other Student's t tests demonstrate that the backed segments are also significantly larger (.02>P>.01), wider (P<.001), and thicker (P<.001). Although no formal test was made, the width/thickness relationship of backed segments and *lamelles à dos tronquées* is shown by the indices (183 and 216) to be somewhat different: the latter are considerably flatter for their width than the former. Backed segments and *lamelles à dos tronquées* do not differ significantly in frequencies of either heavy backing or bidirectional backing.

It is evident that the results of the comparisons mentioned above are not as clear as might be wished. In terms of metrical dimensions, the backed segments are significantly different from both of the known finished tool forms, and any interpretation is thus rendered difficult. In terms of the four discrete attributes available for the comparison, the segments differ from the complete Gravettes in one and from the *lamelles à dos tronquées* in two. Perhaps this indicates more typological difference between the segments and the *lamelles à dos tronquées* than between the segments and the complete Gravettes. Moreover, in spite of differing absolute size, the width/thickness relationship of the segments is clearly closer to that of the Gravettes than to that of the *lamelles à dos tronquées*. Therefore, it is the conclusion of this study that most if not all of the backed segments may most reasonably be considered as medial fragments of Gravette points. (If this is correct, the difference between the dimensions of the complete tool and the medial fragments could indicate simply that it was the wider and thicker—more robust—tools that more often survived in an unbroken state.) Some segments may indeed be *lamelles à dos* (pieces from which one or both retouched truncated ends have been broken off, or pieces that were never truncated), but even if this were certain, there is no way, given the close typological resemblance between the two tool classes, to make a separation on a piece-by-piece basis.

A further interpretation of the comparisons discussed above is to say that the *lamelles à dos tronquées* are not sufficiently similar to the portion of Gravette points to which they are most closely analogous (i.e., segments) to justify the inference that they represent a secondary use of broken Gravettes. If they really were reworked Gravettes, their attributes would be essentially indistinguishable from unreworked broken Gravettes except for the reworking (retouched truncations), and this is clearly not the case. In short, the foregoing analysis seems to indicate that the *lamelles à dos tronquées* represent a distinct tool form not related sequentially to Gravette points.

THE PLACE OF PARTIALLY AND IRREGULARLY BACKED PIECES IN THE BACKED TOOL SERIES

About one-half (n = 22) of the partially backed pieces in Level 3 are very probably unfinished Gravette points or Gravettes broken in manufacture. The backing of these pieces has been started from one or the other extremity and has been worked toward the middle region of the edge. The point where the backing ceases along the edge is usually a smooth, shallow curve, although it may form a more abruptly curved shoulder. The edge opposite the backing at the extremity is rarely retouched. When such retouch is present at the proximal extremity, it is sometimes recognizable as a distinctive Gravette retouched butt treatment (fig. 11, no. 6). One piece is gibbous (fig. 11, no. 15). When partial backing starting from the distal extremity forms a low or medium angle with the long axis of the piece, and when the edge opposite the backing is not retouched to form a distinctive Gravette point treatment, it may be difficult to decide whether the piece in question is really a partially backed bladelet or a very obliquely truncated bladelet (fig. 23, nos. 18–20).

A small number of partially and irregularly backed, non-pointed pieces (n = 7) fall into a miscellaneous category not demonstrably related to Gravette points or to *lamelles à dos tronquées*. These include three with irregular backing (one blade and two bladelets) and four with miscellaneous partial backing (two blades and two bladelets). There are also three *lames à dos* (literally, "backed blades") and five *lamelles à dos*; these are regularly backed but unpointed pieces.

The remainder of the partially backed pieces in Level 3 are shouldered bladelets (*lamelles à cran*). Of these pieces, six have at one extremity the natural proximal extremity of the blank and at the other end an unmodified broken surface. Four pieces (fig. 11, no. 13) have the natural distal extremity opposed to a break. On all of them, the partial backing affects the middle region of one edge, is interrupted by a break, and does not reach the natural extremity of the blank. The point at which the backing ceases along the edge is usually an abruptly curved shoulder. These ten pieces have their *morphological* equivalents in the Proto-Magdalenian backed tool series of Level 2 at the Abri Pataud. In the latter, they are designated "proximal discards" and "distal discards" and are considered to be byproducts of the segmented backed bladelet technique. The quantitatively most important finished tool element produced by this technique in Level 2 is a piece that is typologically a *lamelle à dos tronquée*. The possible existence of the segmented backed bladelet technique in Level 3 will be considered below in some detail.

Eleven of the shouldered bladelets in Level 3 are segments terminating in unmodified breaks at both extremities. On nine of them, the partial backing is terminated by a break (fig. 11, no. 12) or a pseudo-burin removal (fig. 11, no. 14) toward the distal end; on the others, the backing is interrupted toward the proximal end. The point where the backing stops is usually an abruptly curved shoulder. Except for the absence of the natural extremity of the blank, these shouldered segments are morphologically similar to the pieces discussed in the previous paragraph.

Finally, then, there is one partially backed bladelet (fig. 11, no. 8) on which the natural distal extremity is present and on which the partial backing affects the middle region of the edge only. The proximal end is broken, but the break is very near the bulb. This could be considered simply as a bladelet with miscellaneous partial backing if it did not bear a certain resemblance to a Level 2 *lamelle* that is considered to be a backed bladelet not yet segmented. For the purpose of the following analysis, it is included with the shouldered bladelet series.

The shouldered bladelets in Level 3 have a mean width of 5.64 ± .27 mm and a mean thickness of 2.86 ± .19 mm. The width/thickness index is 197. Attributes of the backing are present in the following frequencies:

bidirectional backing	18.18%
heavy backing	68.18%
triangular cross-section	59.09%

Dorsal backing and light backing are absent.

On morphological criteria, the shouldered bladelets could be considered *either* as Gravette points broken in manufacture or as byproducts of the segmented backed bladelet technique for the production of *lamelles à dos*. A comparison of their attributes (see table 17) was made with those of the Gravette segments, on the one hand, and the *lamelles à dos tronquées*, on the other hand. The mean width of the shouldered bladelets is significantly narrower than that of the *lamelles à dos tronquées* (Student's t test: P = approximately .001) and significantly wider than that of the Gravette segments (Student's t test: .01>P>.001). In width also they fall intermediate between the two other samples, but these differences fail to attain the .05 level of significance. In terms of the discrete attributes of the backing, the shouldered bladelets have no significant differences from the *lamelles à dos tronquées*. They do, however, have significantly lower frequencies of bidirectional backing (Chi-square = 12.22; df = 1; P<.005) and triangular cross-section (Fisher's Exact Test: P = .012) than those of Gravette segments.

Once again, the evidence is less clear than one could wish. Small sample size for all but the Gravette segments means that the sampling error is large and that it is correspondingly difficult to demonstrate significant difference, especially for discrete attributes. Nevertheless, it seems clear, both from table 17 and from the tests described above, that the shouldered bladelets are more like the *lamelles à dos tronquées* than they are like the Gravette segments. If one acts upon this finding and groups the shouldered bladelets with the *lamelles à dos tronquées*, the combined sample is significantly different from Gravette segments in terms of *all* applicable attributes. Thus, shouldered bladelets and *lamelles à dos tronquées* are closely similar, but they differ, in combination or singly, from Gravette segments; this is precisely what one would expect to find if the shouldered bladelets were in fact byproducts of *lamelles à dos* production. To be more specific, the weight of the evidence presented so far—morphology, standard typology, and detailed attribute analysis—suggests that what has been described as the segmented backed bladelet technique for the production of *lamelles à dos* is present in the Level 3 backed tool series.

At this point, the objection might be raised that the mere presence of a few *lamelles à dos tronquées* in a backed tool series consisting predominantly of Gravette points does not necessarily signal the presence of the segmented backed bladelet technique, particularly in view of the very small number of proximal and distal discards. The objection would continue to state that the latter, and even more so the shouldered segments, could possibly be Gravette points broken in manufacture and that a larger sample is needed to attest to the presence of the specialized production technique.

In answer to this objection, one can call upon evidence from backed tool series other than that of Level 3. It will be remembered that in Level 5 *lamelles à dos tronquées* are virtually nonexistent. They are present only in the later units of Level 5 and even there they are very rare. The maximum frequency in any unit is five (0.49% of the total graphed assemblage). These five, found in REAR:UPPER, are very varied, indeed miscellaneous tools, and they do not in any sense form a consistent typological series like those of Level 3. In all of Level 5, there is only one piece (again in REAR:UPPER) that might, very dubiously, be called a proximal discard. No other partially or miscellaneously backed pieces raise the slightest suggestion of the presence of the segmented backed bladelet technique. There are some *pièces à cran* that are segments, but, unlike on the shouldered segments of Level 3, the partial backing almost always meets the edge in a smooth line rather than in an abruptly curved shoulder. In brief, in the Level 5 backed tool series, which contains almost 1,500 Gravette points and, relatively speaking, almost no *lamelles à dos tronquées*, pieces that are morphologically similar to the byproduct pieces of Level 2 simply do not exist. Such pieces in Level 3 *could* be related to Gravette points, but the Level 5 evidence argues against this interpretation.

In Level 2, where the *lamelles à dos* produced by the segmented backed bladelet technique account for essentially the entire backed tool series and where Gravette points are totally absent, there are 160 *lamelles à dos tronquées*, 56 proximal discards, and 40 distal discards. In Level 3, there are 14 *lamelles à dos tronquées*, six proximal discards, and four distal discards. It is apparent that the proportion of finished tools to distinctive byproducts (shouldered segments are present in Level 2, but we are here dealing only with the more distinctive extremities) in the two levels is almost identical. Indeed, the frequency differences between the two levels are far from significant, either for discards vs. finished tools (Chi-square = .16; df = 1; .75>P>.50) or for proximal vs. distal discards (Chi-square = .06; df = 1; .90>P>.75). The number of byproduct pieces in Level 3 is indeed small, but—based on the Level 2 analogy—it is in line with the number of finished end products.

In summary, then, the following can be said: The backed tool series of Level 3 consists predominantly of Gravette points. Pieces that were left unfinished or were broken in manufacture indicate that they were customarily made by the same technique used to make Gravette points in Level 5, namely, the backing was started at one extremity or the other and was worked toward the center of the piece. There is, however, another kind of backed tool in Level 3, the *lamelle à dos tronquée,* which is quantitatively of very minor importance. The characteristics of these pieces and of other pieces identified as byproducts of their manufacture indicate that they were made by the same technique that was used to make *lamelles à dos tronquées* in Level 2, namely, the backing was started in the middle of the piece and was worked toward but seldom completely to the extremities. The Level 3 backed

tool series is characteristically one of Gravette points, but the presence of the segmented backed bladelet technique, quantitatively feeble as it is, is important. It represents a clear difference in backed tool typology and technology between the Périgordian IV and the Périgordian VI. Furthermore, it demonstrates that at the Abri Pataud the segmented backed bladelet technique was known and used prior to the time of the Proto-Magdalenian occupation, although only in the latter did it become quantitatively important.

V

Attribute Analysis of Burins from Level 3

In addition to the descriptive presentation of the Level 3 series, comparisons are made here between the latter and the Level 5 burins. Based on these comparisons, we will attempt to make some general statements about Upper Périgordian burins and the functional significance of various attributes. Differences and similarities in *other* attributes among the burin "technotypes" that are based on differences in the nature of the spall removal surface (SRS) will receive special attention.

Inspection of the Level 3 sample reveals no immediately obvious groupings beyond the technical division into dihedral burins, truncation burins, and so on (figs. 12–17), and even these groupings are blurred by the presence of pieces manufactured by a combination of techniques. Nevertheless, the combination of techniques does not seem to produce burins intermediate in other respects; a truncation burin with dihedral modification remains essentially a truncation burin (fig. 16, no. 5).

During the course of the analysis, a distributional anomaly in the lateral position of dihedral burins was noted. In the later units of Level 5, median dihedral burins comprise the modal class, with decreasing frequencies of asymmetrical and lateral pieces. In Level 3, on the other hand, almost all dihedral burins are either median (fig. 16, no. 12) or lateral (fig. 15, no.5: right), with very few asymmetrical specimens. This is precisely the kind of departure from a "nor-mal" distribution that may indicate the presence of distinct types within the general grouping. Further investigation and comparison supported the separation of Level 3 dihedral burins into two types, not exactly congruent with the median-lateral distinction. Assignment to the types was made by a comparison of the median and lateral specimens in terms of other attributes, including the burin angle and the burin edge width. Problematical pieces were integrated with the series that they most closely resembled in the other attributes. The two types of dihedral burins are termed "median" and "lateral" in spite of the lack of perfect correspondence between these attributes and the types thus distinguished. "Median" and "lateral" represent norms from which there is some variation.

The "median" type includes six lateral and two asymmetrical pieces, but five of the former are extremely difficult to orient, and the lateral designation may be a misnomer. The "lateral" type includes four asymmetrical pieces (fig. 14, no. 3: proximal) and three median pieces on which the burin edges have been worked back to a median position by resharpening. These pieces remain morphologically lateral. To avoid complications, no vague intermediate group has been created; all dihedral burins have been placed into one or the other type, and these types will be treated independently in much of the following analysis.

Figure 12. LEVEL 3 BURINS AND COMBINATION TOOLS

SRS TYPE, AND ANGLE

Retouched Truncation

1	(1283): 80°	18	(806): 70°
2	(789): 90°	19	(504): 70°
3	(735): 60°	20	(784): 70°
4	(1065): 90°	21	(1514): 70°
5	(1634): 80°		
6	(1259): 80°		
7	(2206): 70°		
8	(2822): 70°		
9	(2945): 70°		
10	(2737): 80°		
11	(1725): 60°		
12	(1847): 80°		
13	(961): 60°		
14	(1870): 50°		
15	(1643): A: 80°; C: 60°		
16	(72): 70°		
17	(4436): 60°		

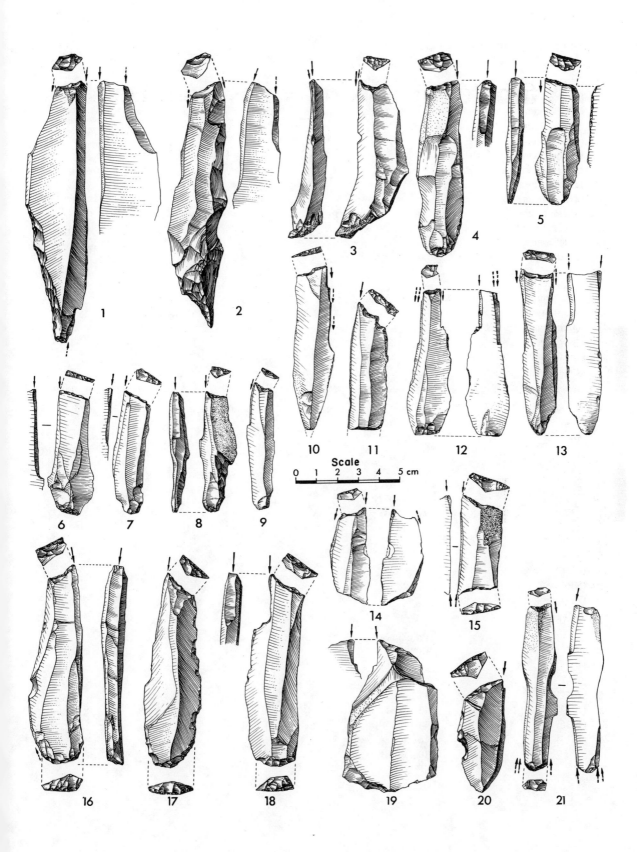

Scale
0 1 2 3 4 5 cm

Figure 12 (continued).

BURIN-EDGE SHAPE AND WIDTH

Straight

1 (6283): 4 mm
2 (789): 2 mm
3 (735): 2 mm
5 (1634): 4 mm
6 (1259): 3 mm
7 (2206): 3 mm
8 (2822): 2 mm
9 (2945): 1 mm
10 (2737): 2 mm
11 (1725): 2 mm
12 (1847): 5 mm
13 (961): 3 mm
14 (1870): 3 mm
15 (1643): A: 3 mm;
    C: 2 mm
16 (72): 4 mm
17 (4436): 4 mm
18 (806): 4 mm
19 (504): 5 mm
20 (784): 3 mm
21 (1514): 4 mm

Irregular

4 (1065): 4 mm

OBLIQUITY

Lateral

3 (735)
4 (1065)
5 (1634)
8 (2822)
9 (2945)
10 (2737)
11 (1725)
12 (1847)
15 (1643): C
16 (72)
17 (4436)
18 (806)
20 (784)

Oblique

1 (1283)
2 (789)
6 (1259)
7 (2206)
14 (1870)
15 (1673): A
19 (504)
21 (1514)

High Oblique

13 (961)

SRS SHAPE

Concave

1 (1283)
2 (789)
8 (2822)
15 (1643): A and C
17 (4436)
21 (1514)

Pronounced Concave

3 (735)
9 (2945)
11 (1725)
13 (961)
14 (1870)
16 (72)
18 (806)

Pronounced Convex

20 (784)

Straight

4 (1065)
5 (1634)
6 (1259)
7 (2206)
10 (2737)
12 (1847)
19 (504)

Figure 12 (continued).

LATERAL POSITION

Left Lateral	Left Asymmetrical	Right Lateral
3　(735)	9　(2945)	1　(1283)
5　(1634)	11　(1725)	2　(789)
6　(1259)	17　(4436)	4　(1065)
7　(2206)	18　(806)	10　(2737)
8　(2822)	19　(504)	12　(1847)
13　(961)		14　(1870)
15　(1643): A		15　(1643): C
		16　(72)
		20　(784)
		21　(1514)

ASSOCIATION OF TOOLS

Double

15　(1643): Retouched
　　truncation

Combination

2　(789) + Truncation borer at proximal extremity
16　(72) + End-scraper (damaged; not included in
　　studied sample) at bottom
17　(4436) + End-scraper (irregular; steep; non-convergent) at bottom
18　(806) + End-scraper (arc of circle; steep; non-convergent) at bottom

MISCELLANEOUS

1　(1283): Worked out truncation burin at proximal end;
　　also very heavy marginal retouch on distal (bottom) portion of left side
5　(1634): With fine inverse retouch on right side
14　(1870): Noailles burin (right margin has recent damage, not a stop-notch)
15　(1643): Noailles burin
20　(784): With deep notch on left margin

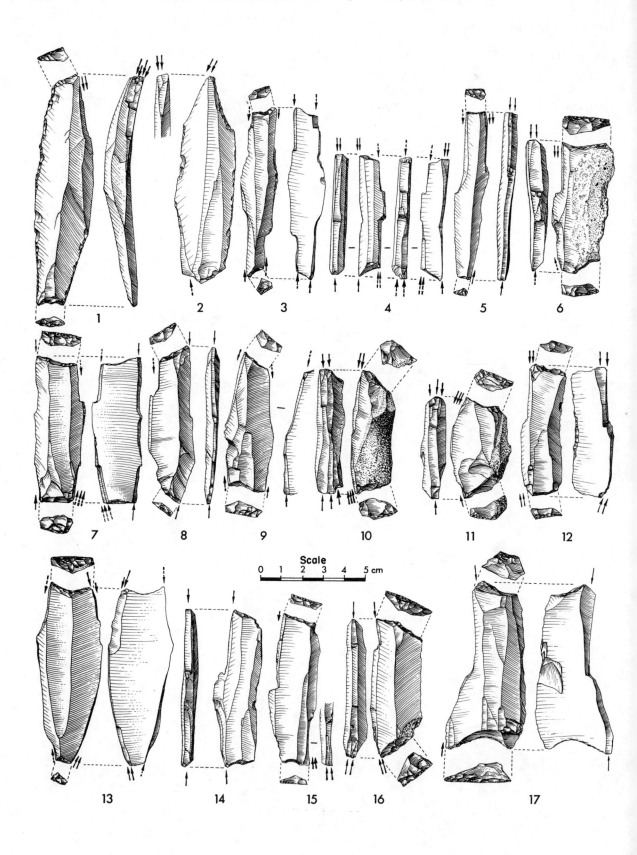

Figure 13. LEVEL 3 BURINS AND COMBINATION TOOL

SRS TYPE, AND ANGLE

Retouched Truncation

1 (819): 80°
2 (116): 60°
3 (614): B: 80°;
   C: 70°
4 (4254): A: 80°;
   C: 70°
5 (2042): B: 90°;
   D: 80°
6 (201): 70°
7 (57): A: 80°;
   C: 70°
8 (273): B: 70°;
   D: 60°
9 (2942): A: 70°;
   D: 80°
10 (1468): A: 80°;
   C: 70°
11 (1608): A: 70°;
   C: 80°
12 (1835): A: 60°;
   C: 90°
13 (647): B: 70°;
   D: 80°
14 (323): A: 80°;
   C: 70°
15 (2082): A: 80°;
   D: 80°
16 (1121): A: 80°;
   C: 70°
17 (817): A: 70°;
   C: 60°

BURIN EDGE SHAPE AND WIDTH

Straight

1 (819): 7 mm
2 (116): 6 mm
3 (614): B: 3 mm;
   C: 3 mm
4 (4254): A: 5 mm;
   C: 3 mm
5 (2042): D: 2 mm
6 (201): 6 mm
7 (57): A: 3 mm;
   C: 4 mm
8 (273): B and D:
   2 mm
9 (2942): A: 4 mm;
   D: 4 mm
10 (1468): A: 7 mm
11 (1608): A: 6 mm;
   C: 4 mm
12 (1835): A: 8 mm;
   C: 5 mm
13 (647): B: 4 mm;
   D: 2 mm
14 (323): A: 2 mm
15 (2082): A: 4 mm;
   D: 3 mm
16 (1121): A: 2 mm;
   C: 4 mm
17 (817): A: 13 mm;
   C: 4 mm

Angulated

5 (2042): B: 4 mm

Irregular

10 (1468): C: 7 mm
14 (323): C: 4 mm

OBLIQUITY

Dorsal Oblique

15 (2082): D

Lateral

3 (614): B and C
4 (4254): C
5 (2042): B and D
6 (201)
7 (57): A
8 (273): B and D
9 (2942): A
11 (1608): C
13 (647): D
14 (323): A and C
15 (2082): A
16 (1121): A

Oblique

1 (819)
2 (116)
4 (4253): A
7 (57): C
8 (273)
9 (2942): D
10 (1468): A and C
11 (1608): A
12 (1835): C
13 (647): B
16 (1121): C
17 (817): A

High Oblique

12 (1835): A

Flat-faced

17 (817): C

Figure 13 (continued).

SRS SHAPE

Concave	Pronounced Concave	Convex	Straight
1 (819)	3 (614): B and C	16 (1121): A	5 (2042): B and D
2 (116)	11 (1608): A		7 (57): C
4 (4254): A and C	12 (1835): A		8 (273): B and D
6 (201)	13 (647): B		10 (1468): A
7 (57): A	17 (817): C		11 (1608): C
9 (2942): A and D			12 (1835): C
10 (1468): C			13 (647): D
14 (323): C			14 (323): A
15 (2082): D			15 (2082): A
17 (817): A			16 (1121): C

LATERAL POSITION

Left Lateral	Left Asymmetrical	Median	Right Asymmetrical	Right Lateral
4 (4254): A	9 (2942): A	2 (116)	1 (819)	3 (614): B and C
5 (2042): D	10 (1468): A	8 (273): D		4 (4254): C
6 (201)	13 (647): D			5 (2042): B
7 (57): A	17 (817): A			7 (57): C
9 (2942): D				8 (273): B
11 (1608): A				10 (1468): C
12 (1835): A				11 (1608): C
14 (323): A				12 (1835): C
15 (2082): A and D				13 (647): B
16 (1121): A				14 (323): C
				16 (1121): C
				17 (817): C

ASSOCIATION OF BURINS

Double	Combination
3 (614): Retouched truncation	1 (819) + Undifferentiated
4 (4254): Retouched truncation	truncated piece at bottom
5 (2042): Retouched truncation	
7 (57): Retouched truncation	
8 (273): Retouched truncation	
9 (2942): Retouched truncation	
10 (1468): Retouched truncation	
11 (1608): Retouched truncation	
12 (1835): Retouched truncation	
13 (647): Retouched truncation	
14 (323): Retouched truncation	
15 (2082): Retouched truncation	
16 (1121): Retouched truncation	
17 (817): Retouched truncation	

MISCELLANEOUS

2 (116): Worked out burin at bottom
6 (201): Worked out truncation burin at bottom

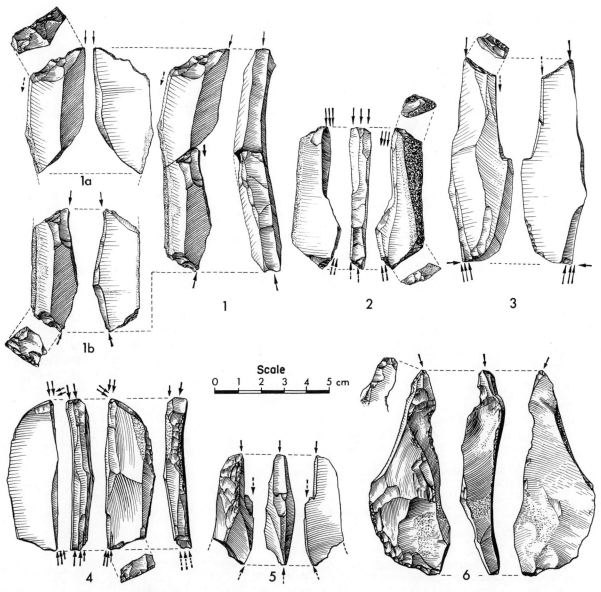

Figure 14.   LEVEL 3 BURINS

SRS TYPE, AND ANGLE

Dihedral	Retouched Truncation	Unretouched End	Retouched Edge/End
3 (250): C: 80°	1a (4991): 90°	1b (4992): B: 60°	5 (3085): 80°
4 (799): A: 80°	1b (4992): D: 70°		6 (1275): 70°
	2 (611): 80°		
	3 (250): A: 60°		
	4 (799): C: 80°		

BURIN EDGE SHAPE AND WIDTH

Straight	Curved	Angulated	Irregular
1a (4991): 5 mm	2 (661): 10 mm	3 (250): C: 11 mm	4 (799): A: 6 mm
1b (4992): B: 10 mm		6 (1275): 4 mm	
D: 7 mm			
3 (250): A: 5 mm			
4 (789): C: 5 mm			
5 (3085): 3 mm			

Figure 14 (continued).

OBLIQUITY

Lateral	Oblique
1a (4991)	3 (250): A
1b (4992): B and D	
4 (799): C	
5 (3085)	

SRS SHAPE

Concave	Convex	Pronounced Convex	Straight
3 (250): A	4 (799): A	3 (250): C	1a (4991)
			1b (4992): B and D
			2 (611)
			4 (799): C
			5 (3085)
			6 (1275)

LATERAL POSITION

Left Lateral	Left Asymmetrical	Median	Right Asymmetrical	Right Lateral
3 (250): A	1b (4992): D	2 (611)	3 (250): C	1a (4991)
4 (799): A		5 (3085)		1b (4992): B
		6 (1275)		4 (799): C

ASSOCIATIONS

Double	Mixed
2 (611): With worked out truncation burin at bottom	1b (4992): B: Unretouched end; D: Retouched truncation (fits 4991:1a)
	3 (250): A: Retouched truncation; C: Dihedral
	4 (799): A: Dihedral; C: Retouched truncation

MISCELLANEOUS

1 (4991+4992): The burin blow creating the truncation burin shown in 1a cut the blank in half, leaving that burin on a positive hinge spall; another burin (1b, corner position B) was subsequently manufactured on the unretouched end of the negative hinge spall.

6 (1275): Note retouch along left margin forming crude scraper (not included in studied series).

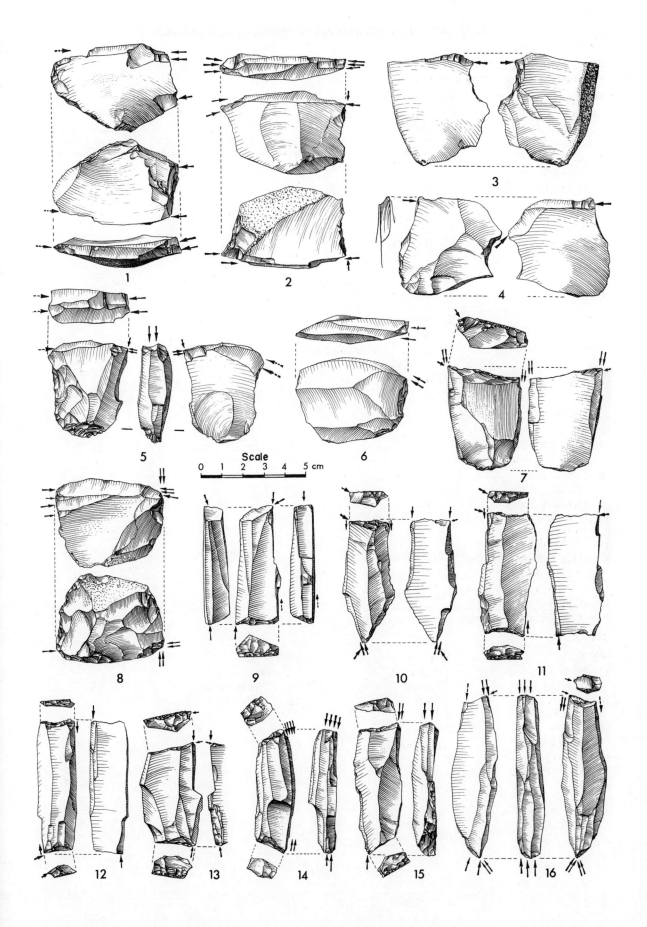

Scale

0 1 2 3 4 5 cm

Figure 15. LEVEL 3 BURINS

SRS TYPE, MODIFICATION AND ANGLE

Dihedral

2 (983): A: 90°
5 (1898): 80°
8 (46): A: 90°
9 (1241): B: 80°
10 (954): Proximal: 60°
16 (1964): Proximal: 70°

Retouched Truncation

7 (220): A: With dihedral modification; 70°; B: 80°
9 (1241): C: 80°
10 (954): A: With dihedral modification; 90°; B: 90°
11 (1826): A: With dihedral modification; 90°; D: 70°
12 (172): B: 80°; C: With dihedral modification; 60°
13 (202): B: With dihedral modification; 70°; D: 80°
14 (629): B: 70°
15 (329): B: 80°; C: 70°
16 (1964): A: With dihedral modification; 80°

Retouched Edge

1 (1905): A: 60°; C: 90°
2 (983): B: 70°
3 (662): 60°
4 (759): B: 40°
6 (846): 80°
8 (46): B: 80°

Break

4 (759): A: 70°
14 (629): D: With truncation modification; 60°

BURIN EDGE SHAPE AND WIDTH

Straight

1 (1805): A: 9 mm; C: 8 mm
2 (983): A: 5 mm
3 (662): 3 mm
4 (759): A: 6 mm; B: 2 mm
6 (846): 7 mm
8 (46): B: 9 mm
9 (1241): B: 8 mm; C: 3 mm
10 (954): A: 5 mm; B: 3 mm; Proximal: 7 mm
11 (1826): A: 4 mm
12 (172): B: 3 mm; C: 4 mm
13 (202): B: 5 mm; D: 7 mm
14 (629): B: 8 mm; D: 6 mm
15 (329): B: 8 mm; C: 6 mm
16 (1964): Proximal: 10 mm

Bevelled

5 (1898): 7 mm

Angulated

2 (983): B: 7 mm
7 (220): A: 8 mm; B: 7 mm
11 (1826): D: 3 mm
16 (1964): A: 8 mm

Irregular

8 (46): A: 9 mm

OBLIQUITY

Lateral

2 (983): A
9 (1241): B and C
10 (954): A and Proximal
13 (202): B
14 (629): B and D
15 (329): C
16 (1964): Proximal

Oblique

1 (1905): C
3 (662)
6 (846)
8 (46): B
10 (954): B
11 (1826): A
12 (172): B
13 (202): D
15 (329): B

High Oblique

1 (1905): A
4 (759): A and B
12 (172): C

Figure 15 (continued).

SRS SHAPE

Concave	Pronounced Concave	Convex	Straight
1 (1905): A and C	3 (662)	16 (1964): Proximal	5 (1898)
2 (983): A and B	4 (759): B		7 (220): A and B
4 (759): A	11 (1826): D		8 (46): A and B
6 (846)	15 (329): C		10 (954): A, B and Proximal
9 (1241): B and C			11 (1826): A
12 (172): B			12 (172): C
13 (202): B and D			14 (629): B and D
15 (329): B			
16 (1964): A			

LATERAL POSITION

Left Lateral	Left Asymmetrical	Median	Right Asymmetrical	Right Lateral
1 (1905): A	4 (759): A	16 (1964): Proximal	10 (954): Proximal	1 (1905): C
2 (983): A				2 (983): B
3 (662)				4 (759): B
7 (220): A				5 (1898)
8 (46): A				6 (846)
10 (954): A				7 (220): B
11 (1826): A and D				8 (46): B
13 (202): D				9 (1241): B and C
14 (609): D				10 (954): B
16 (1964): A				12 (172): B and C
				13 (202): B
				14 (609): B
				15 (329): B and C

ASSOCIATION OF BURINS

Double

1 (1905): Retouched edge
7 (220): A: Retouched truncation with dihedral modification;
B: Retouched truncation
11 (1826): A: Retouched truncation with dihedral modification;
D: Retouched truncation
12 (172): B: Retouched truncation;
D: Retouched truncation with dihedral modification
13 (202): B: Retouched truncation with dihedral modification;
D: Retouched truncation
15 (329): B: Retouched truncation

Mixed

2 (983): A: Dihedral;
B: Retouched edge
4 (759): A: Break;
B: Retouched edge
8 (46): A: Dihedral;
B: Retouched edge
9 (1241): B: Dihedral;
C: Retouched truncation
10 (954): A: Retouched truncation with dihedral modification;
B: Retouched truncation;
Proximal: Dihedral
14 (629): B: Retouched truncation;
D: Break with truncation modification
16 (1964): A: Retouched truncation with dihedral modification;
Proximal: Dihedral

MISCELLANEOUS

Transverse: 1 (1905)
2 (983)
3 (662)
4 (759)
5 (1898)
6 (846)
8 (46)

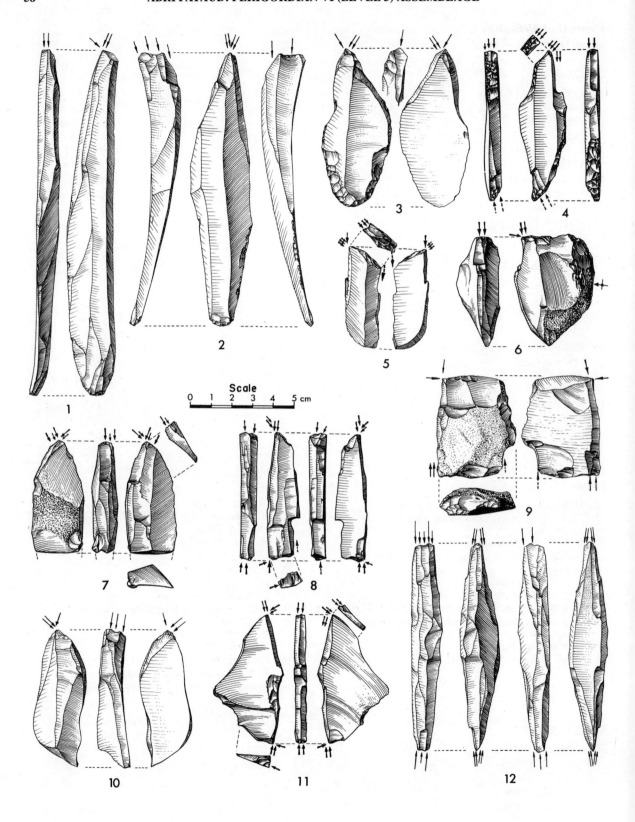

Scale
0 1 2 3 4 5 cm

Figure 16.   LEVEL 3 BURINS AND COMBINATION TOOL

SRS TYPE, MODIFICATION AND ANGLE

Dihedral

1   (4042): 70°
2   (117): 40°
3   (2163): 70°
6   (1271): 90°
7   (1112): 70°
8   (15A): Distal: 90°;
    Proximal: 70°
9   (151): A: 90°
10 (44): 70°
11 (225): Distal: 70°;
    Proximal: 80°
12 (772): Distal: 50°;
    Proximal: 30°

Retouched Truncation

4   (334): With dihedral
    modification; 70°
5   (114): With extensive
    dihedral modification; 80°
9   (151): C: 90°

BURIN EDGE SHAPE AND WIDTH

Straight

1   (4042): 4 mm
2   (117): 11 mm
4   (334): 6 mm
5   (114): 5 mm
7   (1112): 7 mm
8   (15A): Distal: 4 mm
9   (151): C: 7 mm
11 (225): Proximal: 5 mm
12 (772): Distal: 9 mm;
    Proximal: 4 mm

Rounded

10 (44): 10 mm

Angulated

3   (2163): 10 mm
6   (1271): 3 mm
8   (15A): Proximal: 8 mm
9   (151): A: 11 mm
11 (225): Distal: 4 mm

OBLIQUITY

Lateral

2   (117)
4   (334)
8   (15A): Distal and
    Proximal
12 (772): Distal and
    Proximal

Oblique

1   (4042)
5   (114)
7   (1112)
11 (225): Proximal

High Oblique

9   (151): C

SRS SHAPE

Concave

9   (151): C

Convex

1   (4042)
5   (114)
10 (44)

Straight

2   (117)
3   (2163)
4   (334)
6   (1271)
7   (1112)
8   (15A): Distal and
    Proximal
9   (151): A
11 (225): Distal and
    Proximal
12 (772): Distal and
    Proximal

Figure 16 (continued).

LATERAL POSITION

Left Lateral	Left Asymmetrical	Median	Right Asymmetrical	Right Lateral
5 (114)	3 (2163)	1 (4042)	4 (334)	8 (15A): Distal
6 (1271)		2 (117)		9 (151): C
9 (151): A		7 (1112)		11 (225): Distal
10 (44)		8 (15A): Proximal		
11 (225): Proximal		12 (772): Distal and Proximal		

ASSOCIATION OF BURINS

Double	Mixed	Combination

8 (15A): Dihedral	9 (151): A: Dihedral;
	        C: Retouched truncation
		3 (2163) + End-scraper:
		     Distal extremity; asymmetrical;
		     non-convergent; medium

11 (225): Dihedral		
12 (772): Dihedral		

MISCELLANEOUS

4   (334): Former truncation burin at bottom has been extensively modified by miscellaneous retouch.

Figure 17.   LEVEL 3 BURINS AND COMBINATION TOOLS

SRS TYPE, MODIFICATION AND ANGLE

Dihedral	Retouched Truncation	Break	Unretouched Edge	Unretouched End
15 (805): Distal: 60°	11 (1141): C: 50°	1 (9): 80°	13 (1037): 80°	11 (1141): B: 70°

17 (409): C: 70°	16 (1421): B: 70°	2 (1838): With trunca-
		      tion
		      modification; 40°
				12 (1011): 80°

	17 (409): B: 80°	3 (61): A: 80°; C: 90°		16 (1421): C: 90°
	18 (2144): C: 60°	4 (214): 90°		
		5 (119): 90°		
		6 (1015): 80°		
		7 (1882): 80°		
		8 (1559): 80°		
		9 (1528): 80°		
		10 (420): 70°		

		14 (991): With trunca-
		       tion
		       modification; 80°		

		15 (805): A: 70°; B: 80°		

		18 (2144): B: With
		       truncation
		       modification; 50°		

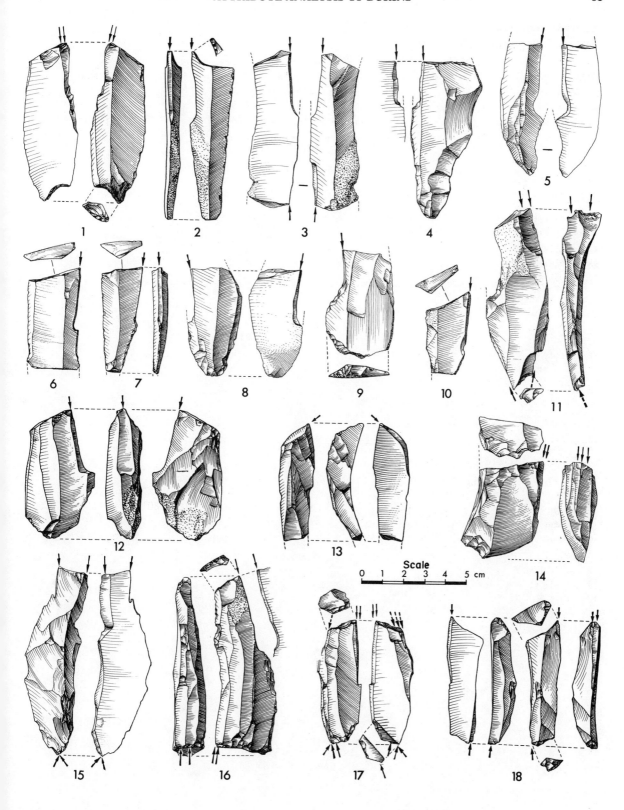

Figure 17 (continued).

BURIN EDGE SHAPE AND WIDTH

Straight	Rounded	Angulated
2 (1838): 2 mm	1 (9): 9 mm	14 (991): 10 mm
3 (61): A: 2 mm;		17 (409): C: 8 mm
C: 2 mm		
4 (214): 3 mm		
5 (119): 4 mm		
6 (1015): 3 mm		
7 (1882): 2 mm		
8 (1559): 2 mm		
9 (1528): 2 mm		
10 (420): 2 mm		
11 (1141): B: 13 mm;		
C: 5 mm		
12 (1011): 4 mm		
13 (1037): 4 mm		
15 (805): A: 2 mm;		
B: 5 mm;		
Distal: 7 mm		
16 (1421): B: 3 mm;		
C: 7 mm		
17 (409): B: 9 mm		
18 (2144): B: 4 mm		
C: 5 mm		

OBLIQUITY

Lateral	Oblique
2 (1838)	3 (61): A
4 (214)	5 (119)
6 (1015)	15 (805): A and B
7 (1882)	16 (1421): B
8 (1559)	18 (2144): B and C
9 (1528)	
10 (420)	
11 (1141): B and C	
12 (1011)	
13 (1037)	
15 (805): Distal	
16 (1421): C	
17 (409): B	

Figure 17 (continued).

SRS SHAPE

Concave	Pronounced Concave	Straight
5 (119)	2 (1838)	1 (9)
10 (420)		3 (61): A and C
11 (1141): C		4 (214)
15 (805): A and B		6 (1015)
18 (2144): B and C		7 (1882)
		8 (1559)
		9 (1528)
		11 (1141): B
		12 (1011)
		13 (1037)
		14 (991)
		15 (805): Distal
		16 (1421): B and C
		17 (409): B and C

LATERAL POSITION

Left Lateral	Left Asymmetrical	Median	Right Asymmetrical	Right Lateral
2 (1838)	9 (1528)	1 (9)	12 (1011)	3 (61): C
3 (61): A		11 (1141): C	13 (1037)	5 (119)
4 (214)		15 (805): Distal		6 (1015)
8 (1559)		16 (1421): B		7 (1882)
15 (805): A		17 (409): C		10 (420)
				11 (1141): B
				14 (991)
				15 (805): B
				16 (1421): C
				17 (409): B
				18 (2144): B and C

ASSOCIATION OF BURINS

Double
3 (61): Break

Mixed
11 (1141): B: Unretouched end; C: Retouched truncation
15 (805): A: Break; B: Break; Distal: Dihedral
16 (1421): B: Retouched truncation; C: Unretouched end
17 (409): B: Retouched truncation; C: Dihedral
18 (2144): B: Break burin with truncation modification C: Retouched truncation

Combination
1 (9): Undifferentiated truncated piece at distal extremity
9 (1528) + End-scraper (broken) at bottom

SRS TYPE AND MODIFICATION

The distribution of SRS type is shown in table 18. Truncation burins (figs. 12, 13) account for almost two-thirds of the burins, giving a "specialized" cast to the Level 3 series. The distribution is very different from those of the later units of Level 5, where dihedral burins are dominant and where truncation burins never exceed 25% of the series. The increase in truncation burins in Level 3 is accompanied by a decline not in dihedral burins alone but in all other SRS types except the retouched edge/end burins. In Level 5, truncation burin frequencies increase through time, so that the situation in Level 3 can be seen as the continuation of an established trend to the point where the dominance is drastically reversed.

Some modification of the SRS occurs on 7.72% of burins in Level 3 (see table 19). In Level 5, modification is somewhat less frequent, and, when present, it is most commonly dihedral modification of the minor SRS types. In Level 3, dihedral modification is most important on truncation and retouched edge/end burins (fig. 15, nos. 10-A, 11-A, 13-B; fig. 16, no. 5). Truncation modification of break burins, which is rare in Level 5, occurs in Level 3 in significant proportions (fig. 17, no. 2).

The retouched truncations, not studied in detail, are steeply worked, the retouch covering the full thickness of the piece (fig. 14, nos. 1a, b). Truncation burins and retouched edge/end burins are easily separable. (This is not the case for the Noaillian burins of Level 4.) It may be noted in this connection that the proportion of retouched edge/end burins does not increase parallel to truncation burins between Level 5 and Level 3 but rather remains fairly constant. Inverse and single-blow truncations are present but very rare in Level 3.

NATURE OF BLANK

The distribution of nature of blank is shown by SRS type in table 20. Mixed burins and combination tools are excluded from the sample; double, multiple, and triple burins are counted only once. Blades are largely dominant, and indeterminate flake/blades are negligible. The blade frequency in Level 3 is higher than in any of the later units of Level 5. Since the frequency of blades increases through time in Level 5, this is another way in which the Level 3 burins continue an established trend. Truncation and break burins are more often made on blades (as is also true in Level 5), and the minor SRS types have the highest flake frequencies. Twelve blanks bearing "lateral" dihedral burins and only three bearing "median" ones are flakes or flake/blades. In general, there is great variety in the blanks used for the manufacture of burins. This should perhaps be taken to indicate that the form of the blank is not especially important so long as it allows the possibility of burin manufacture. Tixier (1958 p. 629) has discussed this point with reference to Noailles burins.

Table 18
DISTRIBUTION OF SRS TYPE OF BURINS
IN LEVEL 3

SRS Type	n	%
Dihedral	60	11.88
Truncation	321	63.56
Break	69	13.66
Retouched Edge/End	38	7.52
Unretouched	17	3.37
Total	505	99.99

DIMENSIONS OF THE BLANK

The blank dimensions of a burin are influenced by the technique of manufacture, i.e., by which SRS type is chosen. A break burin, the blank of which must be broken before the burin can be manufactured, is likely to be shorter than a truncation burin, which, because it is truncated, will tend to be shorter than a dihedral burin. Because burin spalls are more frequently removed down the side of the blank on break and truncation burins, these forms are likely to be more reduced in width than are dihedral burins. Thus, the differences in size between SRS types are not necessarily very meaningful.

The distributions of length and maximum width of complete single burins and complete double and multiple truncation burins are shown in table 21. As expected, dihedral burins are the longest and widest, followed by truncation burins and then by break burins. (The samples of retouched and unretouched edge/end burins are too small to be reliable.) What was perhaps not expected is the fact that double truncation burins are longer than single ones. Since both ends of the blank have been truncated, double burins might be expected to be shorter than single ones. That this is not the case implies some element of choice and selection. Either longer blanks were originally chosen with the specific goal of a double tool in mind, or else when the artificer chose to make a second burin on a blank already carrying one burin, he selected a conveniently long specimen. It is not possible to choose between these possibilities at the moment, but the question will be reconsidered below when burin associations are discussed.

The three major SRS types in Level 3 are longer and narrower than their counterparts in the later units of Level 5. There is in the latter no general trend of change in length, but maximum width of all three SRS types does decrease through time. Comparison of the frequency polygons of length of broken and complete single truncation burins in Level 3 (fig. 18) suggests that many "broken" burins may in fact be complete tools manufactured on broken blanks.

The distribution of near-burin-edge thickness by SRS type (table 22) suggests that there was some selection for thickness. Dihedral burins and the minor SRS types have mean thicknesses greater than 10 mm. Break burins and truncation

Table 19
DISTRIBUTION OF DIHEDRAL AND TRUNCATION MODIFICATION
OF BURINS IN LEVEL 3

SRS Type	Modification	n	% of SRS Type
Dihedral	Truncation	1	1.67
Truncation	Dihedral	17	5.30
Break	Dihedral	2	2.90
Break	Truncation	17	24.64
Retouched Edge/End	Dihedral	2	(5.26)
Total		39	(= 7.72% of all burins)

Table 20
DISTRIBUTION OF NATURE OF BLANK OF BURINS IN LEVEL 3

Nature of Blank		Dihed.	Trunc.	Break	Ret. Edge/End	Unret. Edge/End	All
Blades	n	23	190	39	11	5	268
	%	(76.67)	86.36	(86.67)	(44.00)	(55.56)	81.46
Flakes	n	6	22	6	13	4	51
	%	(20.00)	10.00	(13.33)	(52.00)	(44.44)	15.50
Flake/Blades	n	1	8	0	1	0	10
	%	(3.33)	3.64	–	(4.00)	–	3.04
Total	n	30	220	45	25	9	329
	%	(100.00)	100.00	(100.00)	(100.00)	(100.00)	100.00

Note: Mixed burins and combination tools excluded; double, multiple, and triple burins counted once.

Table 21
DISTRIBUTION OF LENGTH AND MAXIMUM WIDTH OF COMPLETE SINGLE DIHEDRAL, TRUNCATION,
AND BREAK BURINS AND COMPLETE DOUBLE AND MULTIPLE TRUNCATION BURINS IN LEVEL 3

		Dihed.	Single Trunc.	Double Trunc.	Break
Length	$\overline{X}$	76.13 mm	62.45 mm	68.00 mm	55.96 mm
	$s_{\overline{X}}$	13.07	1.78	2.34	2.44
	s	36.98	16.79	16.19	12.18
Maximum Width	$\overline{X}$	29.12 mm	25.03 mm	24.98 mm	24.48 mm
	$s_{\overline{X}}$	3.71	.89	1.15	1.49
	s	10.49	8.36	7.96	7.43
	n	8	89	48	25

Note: Sample values shown are mean ($\overline{X}$), standard error of the mean ($s_{\overline{X}}$), and standard deviation (s).

Table 22
DISTRIBUTION OF NEAR-BURIN-EDGE THICKNESS OF BURINS IN LEVEL 3

	Dihed.	Trunc.	Break	Ret. Edge/End	Unret. Edge/End
$\overline{X}$	10.43 mm	7.95 mm	7.20 mm	12.68 mm	11.88 mm
$s_{\overline{X}}$	.48	.16	.33	.75	1.19
s	3.70	2.83	2.77	4.63	4.91
n	60	321	69	38	17

Note: Sample values shown are mean ($\overline{X}$), standard error of the mean ($s_{\overline{X}}$), and standard deviation (s).

burins are thinner. This variation will be considered again below in connection with burin edge width. In comparison with the later units of Level 5, dihedral burins and the minor SRS types are slightly thicker, whereas truncation and break burins remain about the same. There is a general decrease in near-burin-edge thickness in Level 5, a trend that the Level 3 burins do not continue.

BURIN ANGLE

The burin angle is here considered together with the technique of manufacture, and the interrelationship of these attributes is approached from slightly different points of view. First, the variation of burin angle by SRS type is considered. Secondly, an attempt is made to investigate the possible functional significance of the range of variation covered by the various SRS types. The points to be established here are best made by comparison with the situation in the later units of Level 5. It has been shown that in the latter, the mean burin angles of dihedral burins and truncation burins are very close, but break burins are duller. Retouched edge/end burins are the sharpest of all; unretouched end burins are similar to break burins. In brief, then, there are sharp burins, medium-angle burins (including the great majority of the series), and dull burins.

The picture is somewhat different in the Level 3 series (see table 23). Truncation burins are the only medium-angle burins present (but of course they alone account for the great majority of the series). Break burins are again in the dull category, but they have been joined by all the minor SRS types. When dihedral burins are separated into "median" and "lateral" types, a major difference between the two is apparent. The mean angle for the "median" type is 64.77°, sharper than any other burins in Level 3 or any in later Level 5. The "lateral" mean angle is 79.71°, the dullest in either series. In this attribute, the Level 3 "median" forms come closest to maintaining the norm of the Level 5 dihedral burin (dihedral burins in Level 5 get sharper through time), but the "lateral" forms depart from it completely. "Lateral" dihedral burins, although their distribution overlaps with the "medians," would on this evidence cover a part of a functional

range that either did not exist in Level 5 or was of very little importance there.

The range of variation of each of the SRS types is very similar, and no one type monopolizes one part of the range. Quantitative variations do exist, however, and they may be studied through the percentage frequency of SRS types plotted by burin angle (fig. 19). It has been shown that in the later units of Level 5 there is a tendency for break burins not to occur at the sharper end of the angular range, where dihedral burins are more common. A possible interpretation might be that although burins made by different techniques are generally interchangeable, there is some preference for the dihedral technique when a sharp burin is to be made. In Level 3, truncation and break burins appear interchangeable. Level 3 "median" dihedral burins, although much less frequent than in the Level 5 series, have a distributional pattern similar to that of the Level 5 dihedral burins. Being concentrated at the duller end of the range, the Level 3 "lateral" dihedral burins closely resemble the Level 5 break burins.

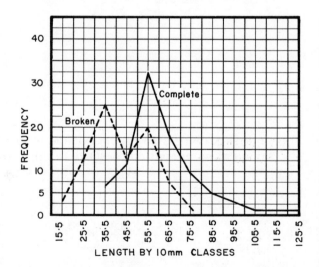

Figure 18. **DISTRIBUTION OF LENGTH OF BROKEN AND COMPLETE SINGLE TRUNCATION BURINS IN LEVEL 3.**

Table 23
DISTRIBUTION OF BURIN ANGLE OF BURINS IN LEVEL 3

	"Median" Dihed.	"Lateral" Dihed.	Trunc.
$\bar{X}$	64.77°	79.71°	70.98°
$s_{\bar{X}}$	2.27	1.66	.62
s	11.57	9.66	11.12
n	26	34	321
	Break	**Ret. Edge/End**	**Unret. Edge/End**
$\bar{X}$	73.28°	73.11°	74.00°
$s_{\bar{X}}$	1.48	1.74	2.55
s	12.27	10.73	10.51
n	69	38	17

Note: Sample values shown are mean ($\bar{X}$), standard error of the mean ($s_{\bar{X}}$), and standard deviation (s).

BURIN EDGE SHAPE

The burin edge is likely to be seriously affected by resharpening, heavy use, or inefficient removal of burin spalls. The relation between the tool as excavated and the tool as a functional entity is therefore more distant than in the case of end-scrapers. This hiatus is nowhere more apparent than in the burin edge shape.

The distribution of burin edge shape is shown in table 24. Straight edges (fig. 13, no. 2) predominate in all SRS types, with frequencies in the 80% to 90% range for truncation, break, and retouched edge/end burins. Nonstraight edges are most frequent for dihedral burins, an important proportion of which are angulated edges (fig. 16, no. 3), but the lower frequency of straight edges for dihedral burins need not necessarily reflect an intentional variation from the norm of other burins. Because dihedral burins are made by blows that form *both* sides of the edge, it is more difficult to produce a rectilinear edge, especially on polyhedric specimens. Angulated and other nonstraight edges are likely to have been produced by chance.

The bevelled edge is a variation from the straight that is produced on pieces with less heavily worked and less steep truncations or retouched edges or ends. It is very rare in Level 3. There is no reason to suggest that the other nonstraight edges are an independent form rather than a variation from the straight due to reworking, heavy use, or mis-striking of burin blows.[2] The majority of burins have been resharpened, often several times, and most dihedral burins are reworked. Angulated edges are the most common variation from the straight, and their widths are slightly less dispersed than those of the other nonstraight edges. The frequencies of angulated-edge widths show no unique internal patterning, however, and in fact the variation in these widths follows the

2. See Semenov (1964, pp. 94–100) for a discussion of burin edge shape.

variation of straight-edge widths within each of the SRS types (see table 25). Burins with angulated edges do not form a coherently patterned group in Level 3. Curved and rounded edges are rare and vary greatly in width, though they tend to be wide. Irregular edges can also be interpreted most easily as variations from straight edges.

Compared with the later units of Level 5, all the Level 3 burins but dihedral burins, which remain approximately the same, have much greater frequencies of straight edges. For truncation and break burins, this difference continues a trend of increasing straight-edge frequency in Level 5. Bevelled edges, which are of major quantitative importance on truncation and retouched edge/end burins in later Level 5, are almost absent from Level 3. This strongly suggests that the retouch forming the SRS is more abrupt in Level 3.

The shape of the burin edge is undoubtedly of major functional significance and should closely reflect cultural similarities and differences in the use of burins. It was even used as the primary differentiator (though not the most effective one) in Bourlon's (1911) classification of burins. Unfortunately, its value as an attribute is much diminished by the fact that many burins have been significantly altered after manufacture by use-damage and by unsuccessful resharpening attempts; such alterations combine to conceal and distort the original intentions of the artificers.

BURIN EDGE WIDTH

The width of the burin edge, like its shape, is affected by reworking. It tends to become larger, especially on truncation and break burins, as the burin edge is worked back into the body of the piece (fig. 13, no. 1: top). Because excavated burin samples include unsuccessfully resharpened pieces along with those that were still functional when discarded, the statistics for the width of the burin edge do not give an accurate picture of the width parameters of the burins used

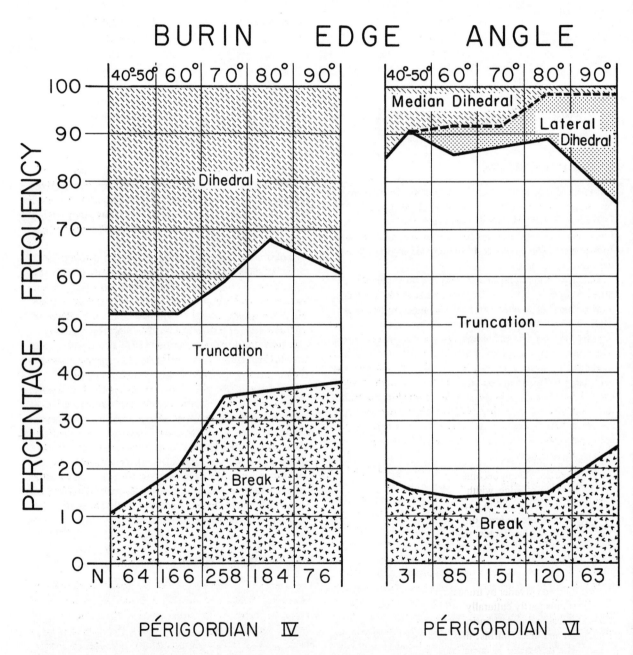

Figure 19.   PERCENTAGE FREQUENCY OF BURIN SRS TYPES IN THE PÉRIGORDIAN IV (LATER LEVEL 5) AND VI (LEVEL 3) GRAPHED BY BURIN ANGLE CLASSES.

Table 24
DISTRIBUTION OF BURIN EDGE SHAPE OF BURINS IN LEVEL 3

Burin Edge Shape		Dihed.	Trunc.	Break	Ret. Edge/End	Unret. Edge/End
Straight	n	31	292	61	31	12
	%	51.67	90.97	88.41	(81.58)	(70.59)
Bevelled	n	0	1	0	0	0
	%	–	.31	–	–	–
Angulated	n	18	14	6	2	2
	%	30.00	4.36	8.70	(5.26)	(11.76)
Curved and Rounded	n	4	4	1	5	1
	%	6.67	1.25	1.45	(13.16)	(5.88)
Irregular	n	7	10	1	0	2
	%	11.67	3.12	1.45	–	(11.76)
Total	n	60	321	69	38	17
	%	100.01	100.01	100.01	(100.00)	(99.99)

Table 25
CROSS-TABULATION OF BURIN EDGE SHAPE AND BURIN EDGE WIDTH OF DIHEDRAL AND TRUNCATION
BURINS IN LEVEL 3

Dihedral Burins (n = 60)

						Burin Edge Width (mm)								
	1	2	3	4	5	6	7	8	9	10	11	12	13	14	>14
Straight	–	–	2	4	3	3	4	4	4	2	3	1	–	1	–
Angulated	–	–	2	1	–	3	4	2	1	2	2	1	–	–	–
Other	–	–	–	1	–	2	–	1	2	2	1	1	–	1	–

Truncation Burins (n = 321)

						Burin Edge Width (mm)								
	1	2	3	4	5	6	7	8	9	10	11	12	13	14	>14
Straight or Bevelled	7	45	53	58	45	31	25	17	4	–	3	1	3	1	–
Angulated	–	–	3	3	1	3	2	2	–	–	–	–	–	–	–
Other	–	1	1	2	–	2	4	–	–	2	–	–	–	1	1

but are instead exaggeratedly wide. Nevertheless, because the bias is in one direction only—edges, except those on dihedral burins, cannot become narrower with resharpening —the attribute of edge width will still reflect differences between burin types within a series and also between series, so long as there are no great differences in the availability of raw material, or other factors that might cause one sample to be reworked more than another.

The distribution of burin edge width is shown in table 26. Among the major SRS types, dihedral burins have the widest edges, followed in order by truncation and break burins. This progression is partly culturally and partly technically determined. Because dihedral burins are more often median than truncation and break burins, they tend to have wider burin edges. The difference in mean edge width between ''median'' (8.81 mm) and ''lateral'' (6.91 mm) dihedral burins is the difference between edges at the thick center of the blank

and those near the margins. But, in addition to this technical effect, dihedral burins are also originally made on thicker blanks (cf. table 22), which implies that the greater width of their edges is genuinely voluntary. The difference in mean edge width between break and truncation burins is disproportionate to the meager differences in width and thickness of the blank. It cannot be seriously contended that break burins have smaller burin edges because they were made on more fragile blanks, which, breaking more frequently and more easily, supplied the necessary spall removal surfaces. The differences in mean width among the three major types are therefore more culturally than technologically determined. The minor SRS types have the widest edges of all, no doubt because (cf. table 22) they were made on the thickest blanks.

Compared with those in the later units of Level 5, the Level 3 dihedral burins and the minor SRS types have wider burin edges. This is congruent with the fact that the mean near-

Table 26
DISTRIBUTION OF BURIN EDGE WIDTH OF BURINS IN LEVEL 3

	Dihed.	Trunc.	Break	Ret. Edge/End	Unret. Edge/End
$\bar{X}$	7.73 mm	4.74 mm	3.80 mm	8.66 mm	8.29 mm
$s_{\bar{X}}$	.36	.14	.28	.79	1.23
s	2.80	2.42	2.33	4.85	5.06
n	60	321	69	38	17

Note: Sample values shown are mean ($\bar{X}$), standard error of the mean ($s_{\bar{X}}$), and standard deviation (s).

Table 27
DISTRIBUTION OF OBLIQUITY OF BURINS WITH STRAIGHT EDGES IN LEVEL 3

Obliquity		Dihed.	Trunc.	Break	Ret. Edge/End	Unret. Edge/End
Dorsal Oblique	n	1	1	5	0	0
	%	(3.23)	.34	8.20	–	–
Lateral	n	23	104	28	9	9
	%	(74.19)	35.62	45.90	(29.03)	(75.00)
Oblique	n	6	160	22	18	2
	%	(19.35)	54.80	36.07	(58.06)	(16.67)
High Oblique	n	1	25	6	4	1
	%	(3.23)	8.56	9.84	(12.90)	(8.33)
Flat-Faced	n	0	2	0	0	0
	%	–	.68	–	–	–
Total	n	31	292	61	31	12
	%	(100.00)	100.00	100.01	(99.99)	(100.00)

burin-edge thickness of these SRS types is greater in Level 3 than in later Level 5. Truncation and break burins in Level 3 have narrower edges than their later Level 5 counterparts, although their near-burin-edge thickness is about the same in both levels. Throughout the Level 5 sequence, there is a general trend for the edge width of all burins (except unretouched end burins) to decrease.

The representation of each major SRS type in several edge width classes is graphed in figure 20; this is analogous to the graph of burin angle distribution, figure 19. Break burins are most common in the small width classes, where dihedral burins are almost absent. The middle range is dominated by truncation burins, and the wide range by dihedral burins. Except for the much greater overall quantitative importance of truncation burins, the Level 3 distribution is very similar to that of the later units of Level 5. Whether or not this is evidence for cultural similarity, it does show some evidence of preference for special types of burins in certain parts of the total range of variation and, further, that these preferences are similar in the two industries. Plotting the percentage frequency of burin types in this way obscures the fact that the distribution of burin edge width, like that of burin angle, is

unimodal in the industry as a whole. With regard to both these attributes, the majority of burins fall within a very limited range.

The functional diversity represented by the differences in distribution does not support the hypothesis that different burin SRS types are functionally distinct tools. It is possible that the forces that acted on the burins between manufacture and discovery blurred the distinctions between SRS types and that if the burins had been in mint condition, the variation might perhaps have been much more marked. Nevertheless, from the data one can argue not the functional independence of burin types but only a limited *preference* for burins made by different techniques in sectors of a functional range common to all burins.

REMOVALS

Straight burin edges may be formed by one or more removals, one removal being the norm for edges of 5 mm or less. On wider edges, multiple removals are more common, with single removals virtually absent above 10 mm (fig. 15, no. 5). Angulated, curved, and rounded edges are, as is self-evident, always formed by two or more removals. Major burin spall scars are often accompanied by minor scars that represent either a regularization of an edge morphology that had been roughed out by the major removals or an alteration produced by heavy use and pressure.

OBLIQUITY

The distribution in Level 3 of (simple) obliquity of burins with straight edges is shown in table 27. Flat-faced canting is almost completely absent, and dorsal obliquity is of quantitative importance only for break burins. Among the major SRS types, dihedral burin edges are dominantly lateral, and those of truncation burins are dominantly oblique. On break burins, lateral and ventrally canted edges are equally represented. The minor SRS type samples are small and difficult to

interpret, but retouched edge/end burins seem to behave like truncation burins. The situation in the latter units of Level 5 is essentially the same, with similar percentage frequencies. In Level 5 there is a major change through time from dominantly lateral to dominantly oblique truncation burin edges. In this respect, then, the Level 3 series is very like later Level 5.

Obliquity of the burin edge may be considered a device to increase the acuteness of the burin angle. By canting the burin removal onto the ventral surface of the piece, the burin edge may be formed in part by the intersection of the dorsal surface of the piece and the burin spall scar, which has removed part of the truncation (or other SRS). In other cases, where the prepared SRS meets the ventral surface of the tool at an angle less than 90°, the striking of a ventrally canted removal produces an edge formed by the burin spall scar and

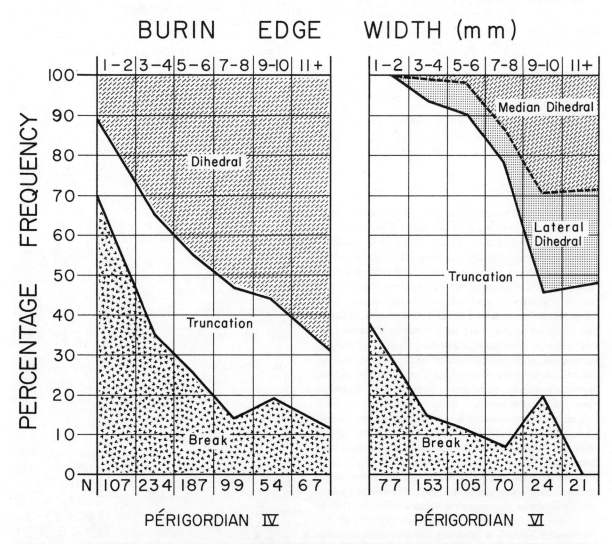

Figure 20. PERCENTAGE FREQUENCY OF BURIN SRS TYPES IN THE PERIGORDIAN IV (LATER LEVEL 5) AND VI (LEVEL 3) GRAPHED BY BURIN EDGE WIDTH CLASSES.

the backward slope of the SRS. In each of these cases or in combinations of them, the resultant burin angle is more acute than in those where the spall has been struck squarely off the side of the piece (i.e., a "lateral" removal). In this sense, obliquity of burin edge may be considered an intentional practice designed to produce more acute burin edges without the necessity of preparing a spall removal surface very oblique to the working axis of the piece.

It is also possible that variation from the lateral may often be the result of slight misdirection of the burin blow. Our own unskilled practice has suggested that an oblique burin edge is often obtained even when a lateral one is desired. However, the very low frequency of dorsal oblique specimens, for which there is no hypothesis of functional advantage, suggests that in general the Level 3 artificers manufactured burins as they wished.

The hypothesis that obliquity produces more acute burin edges may be crudely tested by comparing the mean burin angles of lateral, oblique, and high oblique truncation burins with straight edges. The figures are:

Lateral (n=104)	X = 70.85°
Oblique (n=25)	X = 70.73°
High Oblique (n=25)	X = 65.28°

Even though the effects of obliquity are here competing with variations both in the SRS angle and in degrees of SRS concavity, the figures tend to confirm the hypothesis.[3]

LATERAL POSITION

The distribution of lateral position of burins is shown in table 28. The situation for dihedral burins, with high frequencies in the lateral and median categories and a near absence of pieces in the asymmetrical category, has already been mentioned. A distributional anomaly that cannot be explained either by factors inherent in flint working or by the probable effects of use or resharpening must be considered, at least provisionally, as an intentional effect worthy of type segregation. When the anomaly contrasts with other distributions, in this case those of the later units of Level 5, the evidence for type segregation is strengthened. When the segregates show different distributions with respect to other attributes, the hypothesis of independent types, or at least of functional semi-isolates, is proven.

Left and right orientation are equally represented among truncation burins, and median examples account for 10% of the series. Throughout Level 5, left orientation always dominates over right for truncation burins, a clearly different situation from that of Level 3. Median orientation increases through Level 5, to highs of 10% to 20% in the later units; these frequencies are comparable to that of Level 3. Break

3. It might be claimed that the canting of the burin removals is not so much connected with the resultant burin angle but rather that the oblique orientation of the edge was per se of some operative value. Replicative experiments, which might shed further light on these matters, were not part of the present study.

burins in Level 3 are predominantly right-oriented; this is exactly opposite to the predominance of left orientation in later Level 5.

SRS ANGLE

The SRS angle has a direct effect on the burin angle. If blanks were always parallel-sided, if the burin spall were struck off parallel to the working axis, and if the SRS were neither concave nor convex, then the SRS would be essentially identical to the burin angle. But the burin blow may be struck into the body of the piece (fig. 12, no. 18), the SRS may be concave (fig 12, no. 14), or other devices—such as obliquity of the burin edge—may be employed to increase the acuity of the burin. The direct effect of the SRS angle is thus severely limited.[4]

The distribution of SRS angle (or non-SRS angle for those dihedral burins on which it is measured) is shown in table 29. The lowest angles are found on "median" dihedral burins, the minor SRS types are intermediate, and truncation, break, and "lateral" dihedral burins have very similar, higher angles. Even if all dihedral burins are pooled, the mean SRS angle (54.00°) is still the lowest. In the later units of Level 5, the order of increase is the same, from dihedral burins to truncation burins to break burins, but the Level 3 dihedral and truncation burins have higher mean angles, and the break burins have a much lower one. The SRS angle is further considered below in conjunction with SRS shape.

SRS SHAPE

The importance of the SRS shape is different for the several techniques of manufacture. The advantage of truncation and retouched edge/end burins over other burins is the greater plasticity of the spall removal surface, which may be shaped as required. The SRS of dihedral and break burins, formed by unitary events, can, if unsuitable, only be remade or modified using the truncation technique. The form of a truncation SRS reflects much more closely the wishes of the artificer.

The distribution in Level 3 of SRS shape is shown in table 30. The great majority of dihedral burins have a straight SRS, and concavity is essentially absent. Straight is also the dominant shape for all other SRS types except truncation burins, for which concave is dominant. Convex is of little or no importance except for unretouched burins. In later Level 5, the distributions for dihedral burins and for unretouched burins are quite comparable to those of Level 3. Truncation, break, and retouched burins in Level 3 have greater frequencies of concavity than their later Level 5 counterparts have. The difference is particularly marked (approximately 20%) for truncation burins. Furthermore, compared with those of

4. Correlation analysis of burin angle vs. SRS angle for a small sample of burins of all SRS types suggests that only about 30% of the variation in burin angle is determined by the SRS angle.

Table 28
DISTRIBUTION OF LATERAL POSITION OF BURINS IN LEVEL 3

A. Dihedral Burins

Position		All Dihed.	"Median" Dihed.	"Lateral" Dihed.
Left Lateral	n	14	5	9
	%	23.33		
Left Asymmetrical	n	3	1	2
	%	5.00		
Median	n	21	18	3
	%	35.00		
Right Asymmetrical	n	3	1	2
	%	5.00		
Right Lateral	n	19	1	18
	%	31.67		
Total	n	60	26	34
	%	100.00		

B. Other SRS Types

Position		Trunc.	Break	Ret. Edge/End	Unret. Edge/End
Left	n	147	25	16	5
	%	45.79	36.23	(42.11)	(29.41)
Median	n	33	6	10	2
	%	10.28	8.70	(26.32)	(11.76)
Right	n	141	38	12	10
	%	43.93	55.07	(31.58)	(58.82)
Total	n	321	69	38	17
	%	100.00	100.00	(100.01)	(99.99)

Table 29
DISTRIBUTION OF SRS ANGLE OF BURINS IN LEVEL 3

	"Median" Dihed.	"Lateral" Dihed.	Trunc.
$\overline{X}$	35.28°	68.24°	69.10°
$s_{\overline{x}}$	3.81	2.62	.83
s	19.44	15.27	14.82
n	26	34	321
	Break	**Ret. Edge/End**	**Unret. Edge/End**
$\overline{X}$	71.16°	63.42°	57.65°
$s_{\overline{x}}$	2.07	4.12	5.60
s	17.20	25.39	23.06
n	69	38	17

Note: Sample values shown are mean ($\overline{X}$), standard error of the mean ($s_{\overline{x}}$), and standard deviation (s).

Level 5, a slightly higher percentage of Level 3 burins with concave SRS shape show pronounced concavity.

The quantitative and qualitative increase in concavity of the SRS between the two levels may be taken as a stylistic fact, but it can also be considered as a device that was used to increase the acuity of the burin edge for a given SRS angle. When it is "dug out" and made concave, a 90° truncation (that is, a truncation perpendicular to the working axis) becomes, at the side where the burin edge is to be manufactured, equivalent to a much more oblique truncation. In the Level 3 sample of truncation burins, the mean SRS angle tabulated by SRS shape indicates that shape has a significant effect:

Pronounced Concave (n=89) $\overline{X} = 65.78°$
Concave (n=104) $\overline{X} = 72.33°$
Straight or Convex (n=128) $\overline{X} = 73.38°$

Comparison of mean burin angle with mean SRS angle of truncation burins shows a difference of approximately 4° for later Level 5 and only 2° for Level 3. This means that Level 3 truncation burins are sharper for their SRS angle than are those of Level 5. How is this achieved? Because concavity changes through time far more than does ambiguity, the

decrease in difference of the angles may be largely dependent upon the increased use of concavity. To put this another way, burin angle in the two samples is broadly similar, but the Level 3 artificers did not need to truncate their blades so obliquely in order to obtain an equally sharp burin.

A corollary of these relationships is that concavity should occur mainly on burins that would otherwise produce blunter burin edges, especially pieces with an SRS at or near 90° to the working axis. This was tested by comparison of the observed and expected frequencies of truncation burins grouped by SRS angle and SRS shape (see table 31). Variation from the expected distribution is in the predicted direction. There are significantly more pronounced concave pieces in the 80° to 90° range and more concave pieces in the 60° to 70° range than would be expected by the workings of chance alone (Chi-square=15.51; df=4; P=.004). Below 60° there are fewer concave and more straight or convex pieces than would occur in a random distribution. The large number of pieces that, even so, have 80° to 90° SRS angles but are not concave and the rarity of burins with SRS angles of 30° or less (n=12) demonstrates that a burin need not be sharp to be operative. The use of concavity and the presence of burins with oblique spall removal surfaces show that a low minimum degree of acuity was required.

Table 30
DISTRIBUTION OF SRS SHAPE OF BURINS IN LEVEL 3

SRS Shape		Dihed.	Trunc.	Break	Ret. Edge/End	Unret. Edge/End
Straight	n	51	116	52	19	12
	%	85.00	36.14	75.36	(50.00)	(70.59)
Concave	n	1	104	14	9	1
	%	1.67	32.40	20.29	(23.69)	(5.88)
Pronounced Concave	n	0	89	3	5	0
	%	–	27.73	4.35	(13.16)	–
Convex	n	8	12	0	5	4
	%	13.33	3.74	–	(13.16)	(23.53)
Total	n	60	321	69	38	17
	%	100.00	100.01	100.00	(100.00)	(100.00)

Table 31
CROSS-TABULATION SHOWING OBSERVED AND EXPECTED FREQUENCIES
OF SRS ANGLE AND SRS SHAPE OF TRUNCATION BURINS IN LEVEL 3

		≤50°	60°–70°	80°–90°	Total
Straight or Convex	Observed	29	54	45	128
	Expected	18.74	59.02	50.25	
Concave	Observed	8	58	38	104
	Expected	15.23	47.95	40.82	
Pronounced Concave	Observed	10	36	43	89
	Expected	13.03	41.03	34.93	
Total		47	148	126	321

Table 32
DISTRIBUTION OF ASSOCIATION OF BURINS IN LEVEL 3

		Triple Burins:	
Double or Multiple	122		
Mixed	64	T + T + T	1
Triple	24	T + T + Ret.	1
Combination Tool	29	T + T + B	1
Single	266	T + T + D	1
Index of Association:	60.66	T + T + Unret.	2
Modal Pattern	AC	B + B + T	1
n with Modal Pattern	42	B + B + D	1

ASSOCIATION OF BURINS

The distribution of burin association in Level 3 is shown in table 32. The association index of 60.66 is very high, twice as high as in the later units of Level 5. Over one-half of the double burins are of the AC pattern (fig. 13, nos. 10, 16), the remainder being divided approximately equally among the AB (fig. 15, no. 7), AD (fig. 13, no. 15), and BC (fig. 15, no. 12) dispositions. In the later units of Level 5, the AC and AD forms are equally frequent.

Because the samples come from the same rock shelter, this sharp increase between Level 5 and Level 3 in frequency of association of burins cannot easily be explained in terms of an attempt to economize flint resources or as an outcome of other environmental causes. There is certainly no reason to believe that flint was less readily available in Level 3 times. The association of burins, like combination of tools generally, does help to conserve flint resources, but there is no apparent external reason for this in the Level 3 series. The frequency of association thus appears culturally rather than environmentally controlled and requires a cultural explanation that cannot be supplied at this time. It is true, however, that although there is no regular pattern of change through time in Level 5, the association index is generally higher in the later units than in the earlier ones. Whatever may be the reasons, therefore, Level 3 can be seen as continuing this trend.

One possible interpretation of burin association is that a double or mixed burin is the product of nonrandom association of tools on one blank, each tool contributing to a function achieved by the application of both tools more-or-less simultaneously to the same task. The randomness or nonrandomness of the association patterns in terms of SRS type can be tested by Chi-square. A test of this sort on the double and mixed burins of Level 5 showed that the patterns of association there are not random. Rather, a given SRS type tends to be associated on the same blank with the same SRS type, except that the minor SRS types associate with dihedral burins rather than with themselves. The same pattern of burin association may be present in the Level 3 sample (table 33), as in Level 3 observed frequencies larger than expected are, with one exception, restricted to the diagonal, suggesting a tendency for "like-with-like" pairings; however, very small cell values for this level make formal Chi-square testing unreliable.[5]

It will be remembered that the mean length of double truncation burins (which are the great majority of double burins in the level) was greater than the mean length of single truncation burins. This suggests that in some way or other, the double burin was indeed conceived of as a separate entity at the time of manufacture. The possibility of nonrandom association patterns seems to reinforce this suggestion. None of these data prove that the two ends were used more-or-less simultaneously; sequential use seems much more likely. It is worth noting that there are in Level 3 double burins of which one end is too damaged to be studied beyond the identification of SRS type. Certainly, then, one probable reason for manufacturing a double burin was simply that the first tool made on the blank had been worked out. Nevertheless, the size difference and the possible nonrandom association prevent the too-hasty acceptance of the proposition that a double burin is nothing more than the sum of its parts.

The incidence of the combination of burins with other tools is highly variable (see table 34). The character has no value as a chronological or cultural indicator in the Level 5–Level 3 sequence.

MARGINAL RETOUCH

Marginal retouch (see table 35) is of little importance on Level 3 burins and is not associated with particular SRS types. Level 3 marginal retouch is heavy in the majority of cases. The frequencies of marginal retouch in later Level 5 are much higher than in Level 3, and fine retouch is the dominant variety. Scaled retouch, frequencies of which increase through Level 5 to major proportions in the later units, is almost absent from the Level 3 series.

TRANSVERSALITY

The distribution of transverse burins is shown in table 36. All frequencies are very low, but the most common occurrences of transversality are among retouched edge/end and dihedral

5. The inclusion of multiple burins (i.e., two burins on the same end of the same piece) will naturally tend to intensify the association of like-with-like burins.

burins. The overall frequency of transversality in Level 3 is comparable with values in the later units of Level 5. The distribution of SRS types is also quite similar, with one exception: there are no transverse unretouched edge/end burins in Level 3. The transverse burin on a notched flake, here classified as a truncation or retouched edge burin, is a morphological variant typical of the Level 3 series (fig. 15, nos. 1, 3, 4, 6, 8).

MISCELLANEOUS

Stop-notches occur on five truncation burins and two break burins in Level 3. In some cases the blanks have been thinned dorsally or ventrally by the striking of small flat-faced spalls from the SRS; this has the effect of reducing the burin edge width. In some instances, the burin blow did not succeed in removing a spall from the side of the piece, but its force

Table 33

MATRIX SHOWING ASSOCIATION PATTERN OF SRS TYPES ON DOUBLE, MULTIPLE, AND MIXED BURINS IN LEVEL 3. OBSERVED AND EXPECTED FREQUENCIES ARE SHOWN.

		Trunc.	Ret. Edge/End	Break	Dihed.	Unret. Edge/End
Truncation	Obs.	48				
	Exp.	41.33				
Retouched Edge/End	Obs.	1	3			
	Exp.	5.33	0.17			
Break	Obs.	8	0	3		
	Exp.	10.67	0.69	0.69		
Dihedral	Obs.	16	1	1	6	
	Exp.	20.67	1.33	2.67	2.58	
Unretouched Edge/End	Obs.	3	0	1	1	1
	Exp.	4.66	0.30	0.60	1.17	.13

Table 34

DISTRIBUTION OF BURIN COMBINATION TOOLS IN LEVEL 3

	End-Scraper	Truncated Piece	Other
Dihedral	2	–	–
Truncation	9	4	–
Break	4	1	1
Retouched Edge/End	4	–	–
Unretouched Edge/End	–	–	–

Plus 2 Triple Tools:
   1 Dihedral + Retouched Edge/End + End-Scraper
   1 Retouched Edge/End + Retouched Edge/End + Steep Scraper

Table 35

DISTRIBUTION OF MARGINAL RETOUCH ON BURINS IN LEVEL 3

Complete Singles with Marginal Retouch	5	(3.65% of complete singles)
Broken Singles with Marginal Retouch	4	(3.10% of broken singles)
Doubles with Marginal Retouch	6	(9.84% of doubles)

Marginal Retouch Index: 4.59

Types of Marginal Retouch (Combination Tools Excluded):

Fine	5
Heavy	10
Scaled	1
Aurignacian	1
Flat	1

Table 36

DISTRIBUTION OF TRANSVERSALITY OF BURINS
IN LEVEL 3

SRS Type	n	% of SRS Type
Dihedral	6	10.00
Truncation	11	3.43
Break	1	1.45
Retouched Edge/End	7	(18.42)
Unretouched Edge/End	0	–
Total	25 (= 4.95% of all burins)	

passed inwards, cutting the piece in two (fig. 14, nos. 1a, b). The resulting piece, the top fragment in the illustration, is called a "positive hinge spall" (*coup de burin outrepassé*). Occasionally a burin blow is struck from the distal end of the spall scar, i.e., where the scar exits after having traversed the body of the piece. Such burins have been classified as unretouched edge/end burins. Positive hinge spall pieces are not included in measurements of length and maximum width.

Many truncation burins have old burin spall scars visible on the side opposite the live burin edge (fig. 13, no. 4). This is best explained as having been a means of economizing flint. If it is impossible to obtain a fresh burin edge by simple resharpening, the piece may be retruncated and a new series

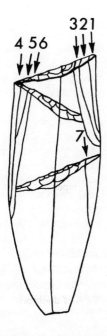

Figure 21. STAGES IN THE REWORKING OF A TRUNCATION BURIN; SUBSEQUENT RETRUNCATIONS AT DIFFERENT ANGLES PRESERVE THE DISTAL ENDS OF SCARS FROM PREVIOUS BURIN SPALL REMOVALS.

of burin edges manufactured on it. If the retruncation is made parallel to the old, it is necessary to remove more of the piece than if it is slanted in the other direction (fig. 21). In the latter case, only a triangular portion of the blank is removed, and the new burin edge is manufactured on the side opposite the old. In this way, the truncated distal ends of the spall scars from the first burin will appear on the side opposite the live edge.

DISCUSSION AND CONCLUSIONS

On the Nature of the Level 3 Burin Series

One of the objects of this study was to test the theory that burins made by different techniques are functionally independent types. The assumption in terms of which the hypothesis was tested was the paramount importance of the burin edge. Analysis of the attributes of edge shape, burin angle, and edge width has shown that, in spite of minor differences among the SRS types, their distinction suggests not functional independence but only limited preference for certain types within sectors of the range common to all burins. It is then legitimate to ask why, if there are no clear differences, one SRS type did not suffice. Because retouched and unretouched edge/end burins are rare and unstandardized, they may be considered residual catagories, individual pieces that for one reason or another were occasional substitutes for the three major SRS types—truncation, dihedral, and break burins. It has been shown that in the Level 3 series, the "median" and the "lateral" dihedral burins must be considered as separate typological entities; this then yields four major kinds of burins. Of these four, the "median" dihedral burins are the most clearly differentiated from the other three, particularly in attributes of lateral position of the burin edge in relation to the working axis and of SRS angle. All dihedral burins also tend to be made on thicker blanks than are truncation or break burins. Unlike differences in some other attributes, lateral position and SRS angle, which are closely related characteristics, are not mechanically dependent upon the technique of manufacture. This is shown clearly by the existence of the "lateral" dihedral burins, which do not differ very much in these respects from truncation and break burins. If the distinctive differences that characterize "median" dihedral burins are not merely the results of stylistic preference, they are apparently giving us information about some kind of functional differentiation within the Périgordian VI burin series. In this case, the position of the burin edge, normally in line with the working axis of the tool, and the overall morphology of the piece, reflected in the SRS angle, are the characteristics that demonstrate the presence of a functionally independent type. Contrary, then, to the premise on which this analysis is mainly based, typological distinctions are not always obviously reflected in the width, shape, and angle of the burin edge. Moreover, the technique of manufacture does not always give the correct functional distinction. The characters that distinguish "median" dihedral burins are such as to indicate that these tools were held and used in a different way from other burins. Furthermore, because it is unlikely that this means only that there were two ways of doing the same thing, the evidence suggests that these tools were employed for another purpose.

Truncation and break burins are much less clearly differentiated from each other—in their overall morphology or in particular attributes. The greatest degree of differentiation that can be observed between them is the limited preference for the break burin when narrow burin edges were required. Break burins, which can be considered either as dihedral burins of which one "hedron" is formed by a broken surface, or as burins on "unretouched truncations," are much more closely related to truncation burins. Their presence in the series may be explained by the principle of least effort. The presence of truncation burins can be explained only by reference to minutiae of burin operation of which we are unfortunately ignorant but which must have made the possibility of creating exactly the right shape of the SRS decisively important.

From this study, some tentative conclusions have been drawn concerning particular attributes. Burin edges were probably all more-or-less straight when manufactured; there is no patterned variation from this norm. Obliquity of the burin edge may be considered a device to increase the sharpness of the burin edge; concavity of the SRS also served to produce a sharper burin. Clearly, however, it was not essential, and it is not even especially common, for a burin to be "sharp." Burins with burin angles of 70°, 80°, and even 90° apparently remained functional.

Burins as the Expression of a Cultural Tradition

The fact that two burins in the Level 3 assemblage fall within the typological limits of Noailles burins does not indicate a close typological relationship between the entire series of burins from Level 3 and those from Level 4 (Noaillian). Although the two burins in question (fig. 12, nos. 14, 15) do not have stop-notches and although they are made on larger, thicker blanks than are commonly found in Early Noaillian series, they are similar to examples from Late Noaillian contexts. In the Level 3 burin series, however, they represent only one extreme of a continuum of truncation burin variation the center of which is distant from any Noaillian norm. There are no major similarities, other than the numerical dominance of truncation over dihedral burins, between the burin series of Levels 3 and 4. Of specific relevance here is the fact that the other burin varieties shown to be characteristic of the Noaillian tool-making tradition—truncation burins with tertiary modification, burin-points, and Raysse burins (Movius and David 1970)—are absent from the Level 3 burin series. (A detailed comparison of the Noaillian and Périgordian VI assemblages will be presented by David in a forthcoming volume of this series.)

The Périgordian VI burins are compared most meaningfully with those of the Périgordian IV. Between the later units of Pataud: 5 and Pataud: 3, there is an increase in the proportion of burins in the assemblage as a whole and a great increase in the frequency of the truncation SRS type. This quantitative difference, analyzed according to the Bordes's system of seriation, would indicate a major cultural dissimilarity between the Périgordian IV and the Périgordian VI, but the only necessary difference is one of economy, for it is economy that is explicitly reflected in the proportions of tools within an assemblage. In our opinion, cultural, as opposed to economic, likeness can be demonstrated only by the typology of the tools, not by their proportional interrelations. The burins from later Level 5 and from Level 3 are taken as a test case. In the following section, the similarities and dissimilarities of these burins will be summarized in an attempt to evaluate the evidence for the existence of a line of tradition between them.

The comparison deals first with single attributes. In many places in the preceding pages, similar attribute frequencies in the two levels have been noted, most inportantly perhaps for burin angle of truncation and break burins (p. 66) and obliquity of the burin edge (p. 71). There are, however, numerous quantitative differences between the two series; some Level 3 frequencies differ from those of all units of Level 5 and some Level 3 frequencies seem to reverse a time-directional trend present in those of Level 5. Some Level 3 SRS types have thicker blanks and wider edges, whereas in Level 5 these measurements decrease through time. The burin angle of the minor SRS types is duller in Level 3 than in later Level 5, another reversal of a temporal trend within Level 5. Truncation burins in Level 3 have fewer bevelled edges, indicating that the truncation retouch is more abrupt. Very major differences occur in the distribution of lateral position, especially of dihedral burins, where a new typological entity appears in Level 3. The left-right frequencies for truncation and break burins are also quite different. Mean SRS angles in Level 3 are quite different, those for dihedral and break burins reversing Level 5 trends. SRS concavity for truncation, break, and unretouched edge/end burins is more frequent in Level 3 than anywhere in Level 5. Finally, there are fewer Level 3 burins with marginal retouch, and scaled retouch is also much less common in Level 3; this again reverses a trend in Level 5.

The differences summarized above are undeniably important—and they cannot be glossed over—but an understanding of the relationship between the two series must be balanced by a consideration of the attributes with respect to which Level 3 differs from Level 5 in a direction "predictable" from trends operative within the latter. Continuity of trend is shown by the following quantitative changes:

increase in truncation burins
increase in blade blanks
decrease in blank width for major SRS types
increase in straight edges on truncation and break burins
decrease in edge width of truncation and break burins
increase in association index

These attributes, no less than the ones for which "discontinuous" differences have been noted, deal with important characteristics of the blank, technique of burin manufacture, and the burin edge.

The internal relationships of the SRS types within each series can also be compared. Within each series, the rank order of blank size of the three major SRS types remains the same, with dihedral burins made on the largest blanks and break burins on the smallest. One of the major differences between Levels 5 and 3 is the diversification of the dihedral burins in the latter level, where the dihedral technique is used to manufacture burins with blunt, frequently wide edges. Apart from their wide edges, these burins resemble unretouched edge/end or break burins in their mean burin angle and might be interpreted as being functionally similar. The differentiation of the "lateral" dihedral burins may be taken either as evidence of the cultural dissimilarity of the Périgordian IV and VI or as an innovation within the tradition that occurred after the Périgordian IV. The general similarity of the "median" type to later Level 5 dihedral burins suggests that the second interpretation is the more likely.

In later Level 5, there is little concrete evidence for functional difference of SRS types on the basis of burin angle beyond the fact that break burins tend not to be used at the sharper end of the range, where dihedral burins are more common. In Level 3, the "median" dihedral burins are distributed like the dihedral burins of Level 5, and the "lateral" examples are most like the Level 5 break burins. In Level 3, break and truncation burins are less differentiated than in Level 5. Retouched and unretouched edge/end burins, which in Level 5 are sharp burins similar in angle to dihedral burins, are in Level 3 blunter and more similar to "lateral" dihedral burins, which they resemble also in burin edge width.

In both series, the shape of the burin edge shows similar variation from the straight (except for differences in bevelled frequencies), and in edge width the same relations are retained among the major SRS types.

The tendency in Level 3 for other burins to be assimilated to the truncation burin in SRS angle is shown either, as in the case of break burins, by direct approximation to this pattern, or, as in the case of dihedral burins, by the "capture" of part of the SRS type. The truncation pattern itself shifts toward somewhat higher angles, but the burin angle is not affected, because increased use of concavity compensates for the higher SRS angle.

Having summarized the similarities and differences between the Level 3 burins and those of later Level 5, the significance of these similarities and differences may be interpreted in terms of three variables: the primary blanks on which the tools are made, the techniques employed in their production, and the typology of the finished tools. The differences between kinds of blanks form different stages of a continuing trend. The dimensional differences are small, and although some represent discontinuous change, others do not. Technologically, the Level 3 series is marked by no innovation; there is not a single Level 3 manufacturing technique, however minor it may be, that is not already present in the later units of Level 5. The use of technical devices such as concavity of the SRS is more developed in Level 3 than in Level 5, but the differences are of a relatively minor quantitative—not qualitative—nature. In the typology of the tools, there are some fundamental differences, including some differences in the manner in which the burin edge is positioned relative to the working axis and other, minor differences in burin edge characteristics. Some of these differences can be understood as a tendency for other SRS types to be assimilated toward the truncation burin pattern. Finally, the different placement of the minor SRS types within the burin angle ranges in the two series has been noted.

In the light of the data produced in the body of this chapter and summarized above, particularly the important ways in which Level 5 trends are continued in Level 3, there is no reason to suggest on the evidence of the burins (any more than on that of Gravette points or end-scrapers) that the differences between the Périgordian IV and the Périgordian VI are any greater or more profound than *those that may reasonably be expected to have occurred over a period of some millennia through internal evolution of a single cultural tradition.* Indeed in the light of later prehistory, it is not the differences in the two levels' artifact frequencies and tool typology that require explanation but the fact that, although separated by a period that must be counted in thousands rather than hundreds of years, the burins, end-scrapers, and Gravette points of the Périgordian IV and the Périgordian VI levels remain recognizably similar.

We therefore conclude that the differences between Périgordian IV and Périgordian VI burins are the product of cultural development. The burins of the Périgordian VI are not the burins of the Périgordian IV, but they can be seen as deriving from them within a continuing cultural tradition. To identify similarities, differences, or the continuity of time-directional trends is not, of course, to explain them. What, for instance, does the variation in SRS type frequencies within the Level 5–Level 3 sequence mean: a change in overall economic adaptation, or the practice of different activities at the one site in question, or something else? Our analysis does not answer such questions. Understanding of the differences between the Périgordian IV and VI is further hindered by the discontinuity of the archaeological record at the Abri Pataud. The intermediate stages within this cultural tradition and the external influences, if any, that may have contributed to the differences between Périgordian IV and VI cannot be identified from the Abri Pataud evidence.

VI

Truncated Pieces from Level 3

The analysis of truncated pieces is oriented toward the distinction of the specimens belonging to each of the three following groups:

a. Tools that should be classed as independent functional types;
b. Undifferentiated truncated pieces, including unfinished tools; and
c. Miscellaneous retouched pieces on which the retouch is at the end of the piece, partially truncated pieces, and broken fragments of truncated pieces.

Because examples in the third group are infrequent and the existence of unfinished tools is hard to demonstrate objectively, the first group, independent functional types, is the most important, and this analysis of the Level 3 series of truncated pieces will be concerned mainly with these.

Comparison of the distribution of truncated pieces by angle and shape of the truncation with the distribution of truncation burins by angle and shape of the SRS shows that the former distribution is bimodal (fig. 22), with the larger mode at a higher degree of obliquity than the single mode of the truncation burins. There is an excess of straight, high-oblique (40° to 60°) pieces, and this suggests that a tool type unrelated to the burins may be present among the truncated pieces.

Study of the pieces under a 10x magnifying glass showed that a number of them have a marked region of wear at the anterior extremity of the piece (the tip) and on the truncation itself adjacent to the tip. This wear, indicated by the rounding of the ventral border of the piece, is limited to the extremity and that part of the truncation adjacent to it and rarely continues more than 7 to 8 mm from the tip. Wear and/or utilization was also found on the margin of some of these pieces, near the tip. Traces of wear and utilization—either on the truncation or down a part of the margin—were found on other pieces, but no other pattern of wear could be distinguished.

The distribution of the pieces with the localized wear described above and plotted on fig. 22 centers on the area in which truncated pieces are overrepresented in comparison with truncation burins. The close association of a particular pattern of utilization and of truncation morphology is evidence of the presence within the series of a tool type unrelated to burins. Three pieces with a truncation angle of 80° show a use pattern similar to that of the more obliquely truncated pieces, but their overall morphology is less regular and, in the absence of good examples with 70° truncation angles, it is

safer to exclude them from the type. Included are three pieces with broken tips, that in their overall size and shape are similar to the group of worn pieces. Also included is one piece that falls within the morphological range but does not show visible traces of use. The total sample of the type, which can be called "truncation borers," is 25.

The illustrated pieces (fig. 23, no. 2, 8, 10, 14, 15) give a good idea of the size and morphological range. There are also two double specimens (fig. 23, nos. 3, 5), one piece combined with an end-scraper, and two with truncation burins (fig. 23, no. 1; fig. 12, no. 2). The characteristics of the type can be summarized as follows:

a. It is made by truncating a blade. The truncation angle is between 60° and 30°, and the truncation shape may vary from straight to pronounced concave.
b. On all but one piece there are patterned traces of use.
c. The truncation intersects with the unretouched margin of the piece to form a point that is usually sharp but may vary from subrounded to angular. There may be *very minor* retouch on the margin at the point itself.
d. The dimensions of the pieces are:
   Length: Mean 73.5 mm; Range 51–114 mm
   Width: Mean 22.5 mm; Range 16–34 mm

Confirmation of the reality of this type comes from the site of Laugerie-Haute, where D. Peyrony (D. Peyrony and E. Peyrony 1938) recognized these pieces as being characteristic of his Périgordian III level but mistakenly considered them to be a form related to the Châtelperron point. They are also present in quantity in the assemblage from Le Cirque de la Patrie, Nemours (Seine-et-Marne), which is related to the Périgordian VI. They are described by Cheynier (1962, p. 82) under the name of "*coutelas*." Finally, it has been shown that truncation borers are present in the truncated piece series of Level 5 at the Abri Pataud.

With the truncation borers removed, the distribution of the remainder of the series approaches that of the truncation burins. The deficiency of pieces in the 70° class persists, but the bimodality of the truncation angle distribution is less marked. It is suggested that some, but by no means all, of the undifferentiated truncated pieces are unstruck burins (fig. 23, no. 11). Several may be excluded on the grounds of size (fig. 23, no. 17), and some bear traces of marginal wear which might suggest that they were used as whittling knives. There are others, with wear on the ventral edge, that appear to have served for scraping (fig. 23, no. 7). Others are not worn and may be unstruck burins (fig. 23, nos. 4, 6). The treatment of the truncation tip on figure 23, number 4, is found on other pieces; there is also a broader, more rounded form and a form with a simple intersection at the extremity between the truncation and the margin. The undifferentiated truncated pieces form an aggregate that as a whole is most closely related to burins. It includes, however, a number of idiosyncratic pieces that do not fall into any standardized grouping. In addition to the 37 undifferentiated truncated pieces, there are 17 miscellaneous or damaged pieces.

CONCAVITY AND CONVEXITY

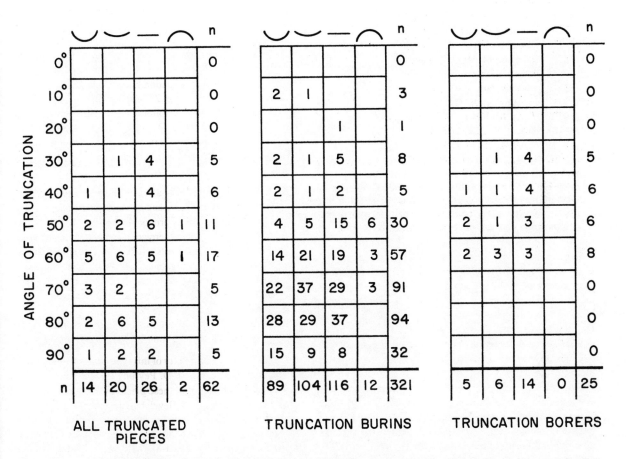

Figure 22. CROSS-TABULATION OF TRUNCATION ANGLE AND TRUNCATION SHAPE OF ALL TRUNCATED PIECES (LEFT), ALL TRUNCATION BURINS (CENTER), AND THE NEWLY RECOGNIZED TYPE OF TRUNCATED PIECES CALLED "TRUNCATION BORERS" (RIGHT) IN LEVEL 3.

Figure 23. LEVEL 3 TRUNCATION BORERS, OTHER TRUNCATED PIECES, COMBINATION TOOL, AND PARTIALLY BACKED PIECES

1 (1800): Combination tool: Distal extremity: truncation borer; 60°; concave. Proximal extremity: retouched truncation burin; 75°; edge shape: straight; width: 5 mm; oblique; right lateral.

2 (83): Truncation borer; 50°; straight.

3 (1013): Double truncation borer; both extremities; 40°; straight.

4 (3713): Double truncated blade: Top; 60ᵇ; concave. Bottom; 70°; concave.

5 (1431): Double truncation borer: Top (broken at tip); 30°; straight. Bottom; 50°; straight.

6 (1200): Truncated blade; 80°; straight.

7 (1663): Truncated blade; 80°; straight.

8 (815): Truncation borer; 30°; straight.

9 (2296): Truncation borer; 30°; straight.

10 (1111): Truncation borer; 60°; straight.

11 (1837): Truncated blade; 60°; straight.

12 (4984): Truncated blade; 80°; straight.

13 (532): Truncation borer; 30°; concave.

14 (174): Truncation borer; 60°; concave.

15 (4970): Truncation borer; 50°; concave.

16 (1170): Truncated blade; 70°; concave.

17 (1442): Truncated blade; 80°; concave.

18 (1630): Partially backed blade (unfinished Gravette point?), partial backing of left edge starts from distal end; obverse retouch on edge opposite the backing at point.

19 (1755): Partially backed blade (unfinished Gravette point?), partial backing of right edge starts at or near distal end; no retouch or utilization on edge opposite the backing at point (extreme distal tip missing).

20 (399): Partially backed blade (unfinished Gravette point?), partial backing of right edge starts from distal end; no retouch or utilization on edge opposite the backing at point.

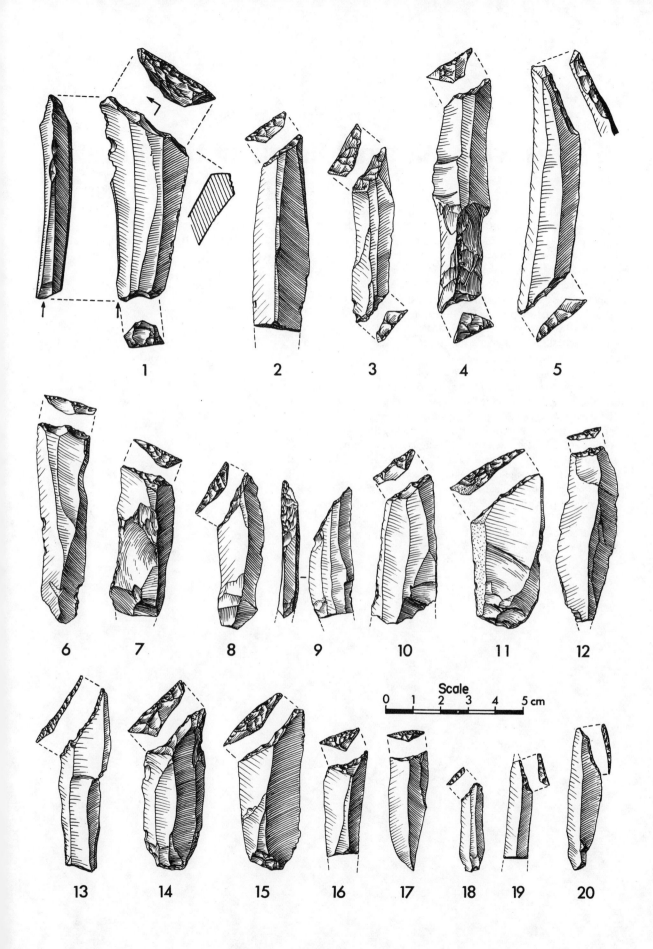

1   2   3   4   5

6   7   8   9   10   11   12

Scale

0   1   2   3   4   5 cm

13   14   15   16   17   18   19   20

VII

Pieces with Marginal Retouch from Level 3

Blades and flakes that are marginally retouched and are not referable to other tool types (fig. 2, nos. 1–5, 7) are very rare in the Level 3 assemblage (28 blades and three flakes). If one counts only those pieces that one can assume to be retouched pieces unassociated with other tool types—that is, complete pieces and distal fragments—and if one limits the frequency count to pieces that are continuously retouched on one or both margins, the total sample is only 14. Marginal retouch is of little or no importance in Level 3, and retouched pieces cannot be considered as a significant artifact type. There is no preference for retouching on left or right margins.

The distribution of retouch types is shown in table 37. Fine retouch is predominant, as it is in the Level 5 retouched blade series. Heavy retouch is more frequent than scaled retouch. The data do not suggest that heavy retouch is especially applied at the butt of tools in order to facilitate hafting or holding in the hand. Scaled retouch, represented by lightly worked examples, is a variation from the fine retouch accomplished by a change in the angle of the blows.

The number of complete marginally retouched pieces, nearly half of which are flakes, is insufficient to warrant further study. They are varied in size and shape, and there is no evidence of any distinguishable independent type.

Table 37

DISTRIBUTION OF RETOUCH TYPES ON PIECES WITH MARGINAL RETOUCH IN LEVEL 3

Retouch Type

Fine		Fragments	10
		Complete	5
	n		15
	%		(48.39)
Heavy		Fragments	7
		Complete	1
	n		8
	%		(25.81)
Scaled		Fragments	4
		Complete	1
	n		5
	%		(16.13)
Mixed	n		3
	%		(9.68)
Total		Blades	28
		Flakes	3
	n		31
	%		(100.01)

VIII

Nuclei from Level 3

SHAPE

There are 397 nuclei or slightly worked nodules and chunks of flint in Level 3 (table 38). The great majority (74.23%) of the 291 classified nuclei have the prismatic form, either elongated, or broad and flat. Many exhibit roughly retouched—i.e., "prepared"—striking platforms. The majority of the elongated prismatic nuclei have two striking platforms, which are most frequently arranged in the opposed pattern. A single striking platform is most common on the broad or flat prismatic nuclei, although on these as well, when two platforms are present, they are most frequently opposed. All seven of the pyramidal examples (2.41%) are small and could have served in the production of bladelet blanks for small backed tools. Although they have been divided into the several shape categories, the Level 3 nuclei constitute a continuous series. The elongated prismatic forms grade imperceptibly into those that are relatively broader and flatter, usually as a result of their having been worked closer to one edge of the nodule. The short broad forms can, in turn, grade into the globular examples. Then follow the irregular forms, the shapes of which have often been determined in part by impurities in the flint or the irregular shape of the nodule.

The Level 3 fragmentary nuclei, two of which have been broken by heat, cannot be assigned to a shape category. Pieces described as chunks (*ébauches* or rough-outs) are nodules that, because of visible flaws in the flint, have been obviously unsuccessful in producing good blanks, although multiple removals have been made. Attempts are nodules from which only two or three preliminary, cortical trimming flakes have been removed; for one reason or another, the process of blank production was never continued.

Some terminological explanation is necessary in order to compare the Level 3 nuclei with those of Level 5. In Level 5, the term "prismatic" was applied only to what is here called "elongated prismatic," and flat nuclei were treated as a separate category. Level 5 globular and irregular examples, which were distinguished from each other in the attribute-recording stage, were pooled in the analysis and were labeled simply as "irregular," because they were not regarded as being sufficiently distinctive. With these slight differences taken into account, a comparison between nucleus shape in Level 3 and that in the later units of Level 5 is shown in table 39. Throughout all of Level 5, there is a marked increase through time in the frequency of prismatic (=elongated prismatic) nuclei; this trend is clearly continued by the nuclei

of Level 3. The frequency of broad prismatic (=flat) nuclei is also higher in Level 3. Tabular nuclei, which have a general decrease in time throughout Level 5, are almost absent in Level 3. The other major decrease between Levels 5 and 3 is in irregular and globular nuclei. Pyramidal nuclei, present but rare in Level 3, are entirely absent in the later units of Level 5. Since, however, they are present (their maximum frequency is 3%) in the earlier units of Level 5, no continued trend in this regard is present between the two levels.

Although almost all of the nuclei found by the archaeologist are likely to be virtually "worked out" and attempts to characterize the blank produced are therefore uncertain at best, the prismatic nucleus, especially the elongated variety, is certainly the classic blade core of the Upper Palaeolithic. A high frequency of prismatic nuclei generally accompanies a high proportion of blade blanks in the tool sample; this is certainly the case for Level 3. If the blank most often desired was a blade blank, the probability is strong that many or most of the now globular and irregular nuclei were prismatic blade cores before they reached their present worked-out state. It might be expected that an increase in prismatic nuclei between Level 5 and Level 3 ought to be reflected in the tool sample by an increase in blade blanks, and our analysis shows that in part such an increase takes place. Although somewhat more flake blanks are used for end-scrapers in Level 3 than in the later units of Level 5, in the much more numerous burin class, it is blade blanks that increase between Levels 5 and 3. Not only are blades more numerous in the Level 3 burin series but they are also somewhat longer and narrower (more "blady"). Thus, the comparative picture provided by the nuclei is in at least partial agreement with that provided by the tool sample.

FLINT VARIETY

Of all the 397 nuclei or slightly modified nodules, only 14 (3.5%) are composed of Maestrichtian (Upper Cretaceous) flint; this flint does not occur in the Les Eyzies vicinity but is found in limestone outcrops in the vicinity of Bergerac (Dordogne). The other 383 pieces (96.47%) are of one variety or another of either Campanian or Coniacian (Upper Cretaceous) flint—mostly black but sometimes gray, tan, or blond—which occurs in limestone outcrops of the Les Eyzies vicinity.

The very feeble representation of Maestrichtian "Bergerac" flint in the nucleus sample is surprising in view of its considerably greater importance in the tool samples.

Table 38
DISTRIBUTION OF SHAPE OF NUCLEI IN LEVEL 3

		n	%
Prismatic		216	74.23
a) Elongated			
With One Striking Platform	65		
With Two Alternate Striking Platforms	20		
With Two Opposed Striking Platforms	72		
With Two Crossed Striking Platforms	9		
b) Broad (Flat)			
With One Striking Platform	30		
With Two Alternate Striking Platforms	4		
With Two Opposed Striking Platforms	11		
With Two Crossed Striking Platforms	5		
Pyramidal		7	2.41
Tabular		2	0.69
Globular		32	11.00
Irregular		34	11.68
Subtotal		291	100.01
Fragments		25	
Chunks (*Ébauches*) and Attempts		81	
Subtotal		106	
TOTAL		397	

Table 39
COMPARISON OF NUCLEUS SHAPE DISTRIBUTIONS IN LEVEL 3
AND THE LATER UNITS OF LEVEL 5

Level 3

	n	%
Elongated Prismatic	166	57.04
Broad Prismatic	50	17.18
Irregular & Globular	66	22.68
Tabular	2	0.69
Pyramidal	7	2.41
	291	100.00

Level 5

	REAR:UPPER		REAR:LOWER		FRONT:UPPER	
	n	%	n	%	n	%
Prismatic	42	53.16	23	(51.11)	52	51.49
Flat	8	10.13	4	(8.89)	9	8.91
Irregular	24	30.38	17	(37.78)	35	34.65
Tabular	5	6.33	1	(2.22)	5	4.95
Pyramidal	–	–	–	–	–	–
	79	100.00	45	(100.00)	101	100.00

Flint variety was not systematically noted for all tools during the attribute-recording stage, but a later sorting of 410 burins and 217 scrapers of all kinds showed that 33.41% of the burins and 23.04% of the scrapers are made from Maestrichtian flint. Without a detailed study of the *débitage* flakes, no documented case can be made, but such a great difference between the nuclei and the tools strongly suggests that a considerable number of tools made on Maestrichtian flint were brought to the Abri Pataud as finished tools rather than manufactured there.

The frequency of Maestrichtian-flint nuclei in Level 3 is much smaller than that in the later units of Level 5 (14% to 20%). The proportions of end-scrapers and burins made on Maestrichtian flint in later Level 5 are also greater than in Level 3, but the differences are not so great as for the nuclei. The possibility of importation to the Abri Pataud of finished tools of Maestrichtian flint was already raised for later Level 5, but if the suggested interpretations for both levels are correct, the Level 3 occupants of the Abri Pataud appear to have brought with them a higher proportion of finished tools on exotic flint than did those of Level 5.

SUMMARY

The Level 3 nuclei, among which prismatic forms are very well represented, are indicative of the quantitative importance of blade blanks in the industry. Almost all the nuclei worked at the Abri Pataud are composed of Campanian or Coniacian flint available locally in the Les Eyzies vicinity. The possibility exists, although it has not been demonstrated, that many of the tool blanks made from Maestrichtian flint of the Bergerac vicinity were not produced at the site. The nucleus shapes in Level 3 are very similar to those of later Level 5, and in important respects, they continue trends of change established within the latter level. The major difference between the nuclei of Levels 3 and 5 is the much lower frequency of Maestrichtian flint in Level 3.

IX

The Nonflint Industry of Level 3

STONE OTHER THAN FLINT (table 40)

Chopper

The single chopper in Level 3 is a large, subrectangular, water-rolled pebble of gneissic granite (fig. 24, no. 1). Large removals at each end make it a double-ended chopper, although the working at both ends is very partially bifacial. Two chopping-tools of flint have already been discussed (p. 12).

Hammerstones

Eight of the nine hammerstones in Level 3 are medium or large, water-rolled quartz pebbles the ends and sides of which show battering and crushing. The modification on some is so intensive that the pebble has been partially shattered (fig. 24, nos. 2, 3). The other hammerstone is a large, water-rolled pebble of granite. This tool and one of the quartz tools (fig. 24, no. 2) have also been used as anvil stones (see below).

Flaking Tools (*Retouchoirs*) or Anvil Stones

The stone tools described as flaking tools or anvil stones bear concentrated areas of short scratches, indentations, and pock marks. The nature of this modification is the same as on the bone tools called flaking tools or anvils (*compresseurs*). One of the flaking tools is an elongated, water-rolled andesite pebble; the scratched and cut areas are limited to the pointed extremities. A flat, water-rolled gneiss pebble has been extensively used as a flaking tool or anvil stone, and also probably as a hammerstone. The majority (n=7) of the tools in this category are water-rolled pebbles of dolomitic limestone. One of these bears purposeful engraved lines in addition to the traces of use as a tool (Movius 1977, p. 52, fig. h); it is described below among the art objects.

Grinding, Polishing, or Rubbing Stones

Two rather different kinds of tools are represented here. Two examples, one of fine sandstone and the other of coarse, cemented sandstone or gritstone, have very pronounced faceting on one side. Each tool has only one facet, extending the length of the stone and worn quite flat. Because of the texture of the rock, striations cannot be seen on the faceted surface. Both of these may be considered as hand-held grinding stones.

Table 40
DISTRIBUTION OF OBJECTS MADE OF STONE OTHER THAN FLINT AND OF PERFORATED MOLLUSC SHELLS IN LEVEL 3

Artifact Category	n
Chopper	1
Hammerstones	9
Flaking Tools or Anvil Stones	9
Grinding, Polishing, or Rubbing Stones	3
Coloring Matter: Hematite	23
Coloring Matter: Manganese Dioxide	1
Stone Bead or Pendant	1
Hand-Axes (Flint)	2
Miscellaneous Stone Tools	1
Miscellaneous Stone Objects	3
Perforated Mollusc Shells	10

The third tool (fig. 25, no. 3), also of fine sandstone, is grooved rather than faceted. The grooves are V-shaped and 2 to 3 mm in depth. It has one long groove, and two shorter ones with slightly different axes.

Coloring Matter

A small series of pieces of hematite was found in Level 3; it included 23 separate finds, some of which consisted of multiple fragments. Among these are 12 hematite crayons, each bearing at least one flattened and striated facet. Most of the crayons are small, but the largest one, with one major facet and several smaller ones, is approximately 55 by 50 by 30 mm in maximum dimensions (fig. 26, no. 3). There is one crayon of manganese dioxide, again with the striated faceting.

There is much less hematite in Level 3 than in Level 5; this is a major difference between the two assemblages. It seems likely that there is also a difference in the way the hematite was used; in the large series from Level 5, faceted crayons of the kind so well represented in Level 3 are virtually absent. Manganese dioxide is of no quantitative importance in either level.

Stone Bead or Pendant

This object is a subrectangular piece of hard, fossiliferous limestone 31 by 25 by 6 mm in size (fig. 27, no. 12). Near one end are two overlapping depressions that may represent

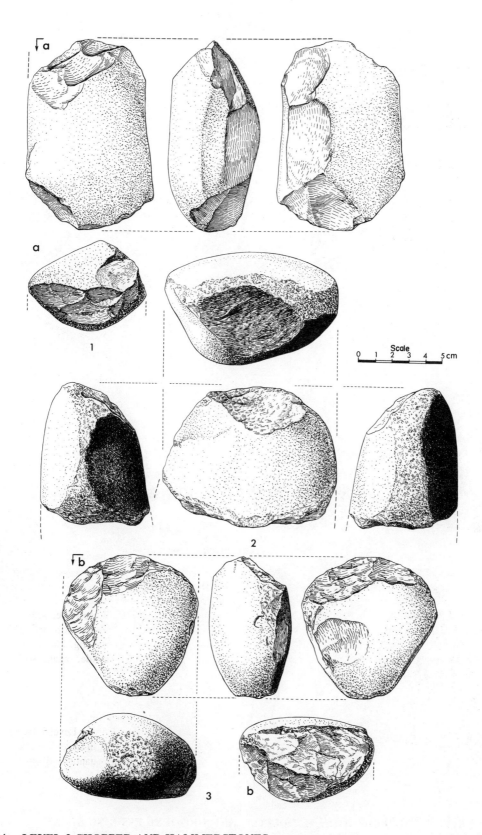

Figure 24.   LEVEL 3 CHOPPER AND HAMMERSTONES
1 (564): Chopper made on pebble of granite (or ? gneiss). 2 (1195): Hammerstone of quartz. 3 (939): Hammerstone of quartz.

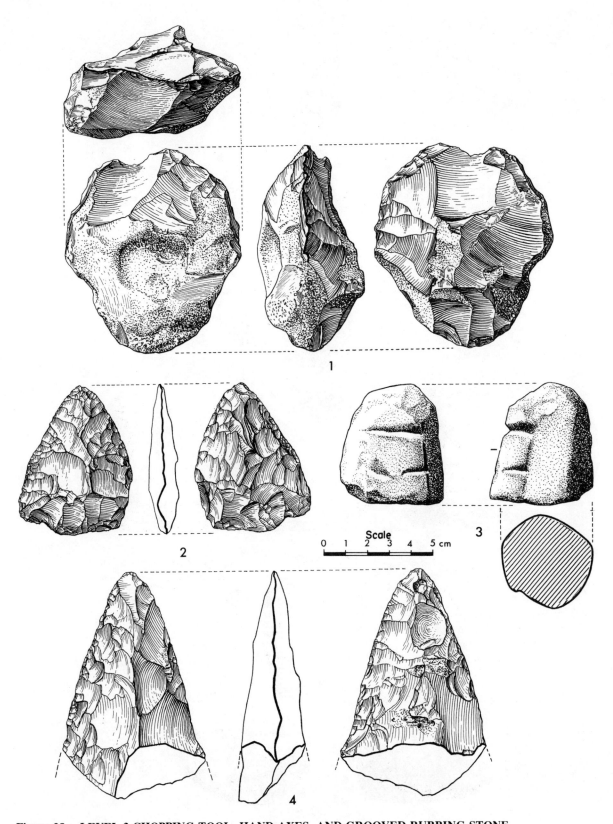

Figure 25. LEVEL 3 CHOPPING TOOL, HAND-AXES, AND GROOVED RUBBING STONE

1 (1076): Chopping tool manufactured on flint nodule. 2 (238): Small, flat, triangular biface, or hand-axe, of flint. 3 (1455): Grooved rubbing stone of red sandstone. 4 (1740): Pointed anterior portion of flint biface or hand-axe.

attempts to perforate the stone. The margin of the piece is fractured just at these depressions.

Hand-Axes

Two hand-axes were found in Level 3. Although they are both made of flint, they are discussed here rather than with the flint industry included in the cumulative graph because they are regarded as "fossil" tools and not as parts of the Level 3 tool kit. One of the hand-axes is fragmentary; it is the distal portion of a large, pointed hand-axe of Acheulian type (fig. 25, no. 4). The other (fig. 25, no. 2), a complete piece, is a small, flat, cordiform hand-axe typical of the Mousterian of Acheulian Tradition.

Miscellaneous Stone Tools

A large oval flake from the side of a water-rolled quartz pebble has a sharp, arcuate edge much modified by bifacial utilization removals. Presumably it was used as a side-scraper or knife.

Miscellaneous Stone Objects

These are stone objects that were brought into the site but are not demonstrably tools, ornaments, or coloring matter. They include a fragment of water-rolled quartz crystal, a small calcareous concretion, and a small, oddly shaped bit of chalcedony.

MOLLUSC SHELLS (table 40)

Perforated Mollusc Shells

A small series of fossil marine molluscs was found in Level 3 (Dance 1975, p. 155, table 2). Nine of the shells are perforated and are considered to be ornaments. These include four examples of *Pirenella plicata* (fig. 27, nos. 4, 5) and five examples of *Typanotonos margaritaceus* (ibid., p. 157, fig. 1, no. 6); both of these are gastropods from Lower Miocene deposits of the Bordeaux region.

A single example of a Pleistocene marine mollusc, *Homalopoma sanguinea,* is perforated for suspension. According to Dance (ibid., p. 156), this species is common today in the Mediterranean, but fragments have also been dredged off the Atlantic coast of France.

Other Mollusc Shells

Two examples of *Cyclothyris difformis* may have been used as ornaments, but they are not perforated. These are fossil brachiopods that weather out of the Cretaceous limestone wall of the shelter. Single non-perforated specimens of two Pleistocene marine molluscs, *Patella vulgata* and *Macoma*

baltica, also occur in Level 3. Both species are living today on the Atlantic coast of France.

TOOTH, BONE, ANTLER, AND IVORY (table 41)

Perforated Teeth

There are only five perforated teeth in Level 3—two of fox (fig. 27, no. 8), one canine tooth of red deer ("*crâche*") (fig. 27, no. 7), one incisor tooth of red deer (fig. 27, no. 6), and one that has not been identified.

Although it is generally similar, the technique of tooth perforation differs in certain details from that used in Level 5. Only two pieces have clear lead-in grooves (fig. 27, no. 6). On one tooth, there are, instead of grooves, irregular polygonal pits from which the perforation was then made (fig. 27, no. 7). None of the Level 3 examples shows good evidence of biconical drilling, but the technique is really indeterminate in three cases because of breakage. One of the two well-preserved pieces (fig. 27, no. 6) was not drilled at all; the hole was cut or punched through the thin layer of material separating the bottoms of the lead-in grooves.

Antler Polishers (*Polissoirs*)

The polishers of Level 3 are made only of antler. The antler shaft has been halved longitudinally, and the distal end has

Table 41
DISTRIBUTION OF OBJECTS MADE OF TOOTH,
BONE, ANTLER, AND IVORY IN LEVEL 3

Artifact Category	n
Perforated Teeth	5
Antler Polishers	12
Bone Smoothers	12
Antler Smoothers	4
Ivory Smoother	1
Bone Awls	23
Antler Awls	2
Bone, Antler, and Ivory Sagaies	38
Bone Gorges	4
Bone Pin	1
Eyeless Bone Needle or Pin	1
Bone Flaking Tools or Anvils	4
Antler Wedge	1
Fusiform Bone Object	1
Antler *Baguettes*	3
Incised Bone	5
Antler Worked by Groove-and-Splinter Technique	15
Miscellaneous Worked Bone	6
Miscellaneous Worked Antler	8
Miscellaneous Worked Ivory	2

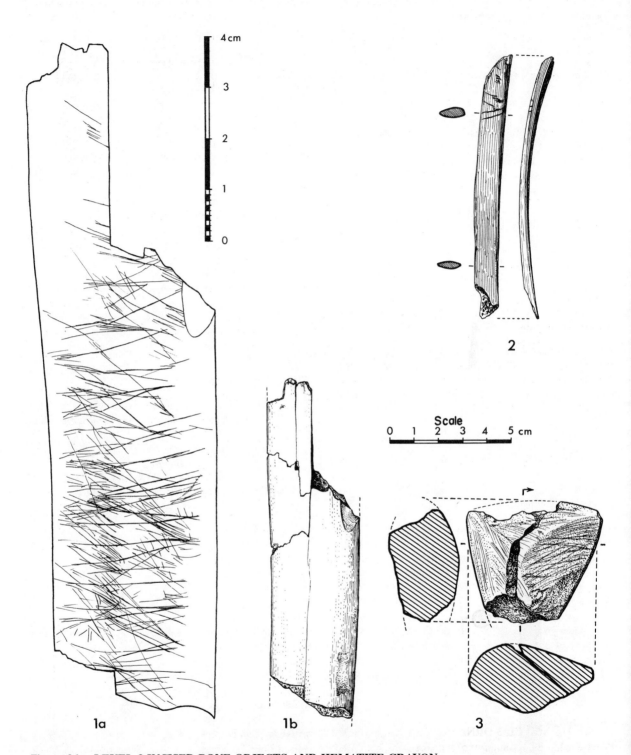

Figure 26. LEVEL 3 INCISED BONE OBJECTS AND HEMATITE CRAYON

1a + b (292): Fragment of large rib (13.3 cm long) broken at both extremities and with incisions on the upper surface; 1a = × 2; 1b = natural size. 2 (608): Fragment of small rib with two incised parallel lines at one extremity. 3 (1459): Red ochre (hematite) crayon with striations resulting from use.

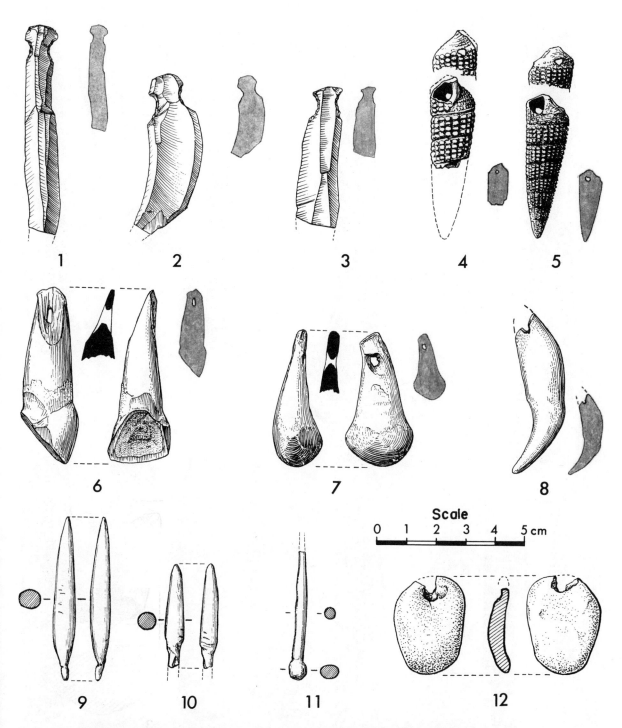

Figure 27. LEVEL 3 ORNAMENTS OF VARIOUS KINDS AND POSSIBLE GORGE
1 (415): Flint "pendeloque." 2 (894): Flint "pendeloque." 3 (893): Flint "pendeloque." 4 (657): Pierced fossil shell from Gironde—of Lower Miocene Age. 5 (519): Pierced fossil shell from Gironde—of Lower Miocene Age. 6 (1016): Perforated red deer incisor. 7 (1162): Perforated red deer canine. 8 (1546): Perforated fox canine. 9 (330): Fusiform-shaped bone object—? pendant. 10 (1206): Bone object—probably a "gorge" (hameçon). 11 (24): Bone pin with head. 12 (426): Stone bead or pendant; broken at perforation.

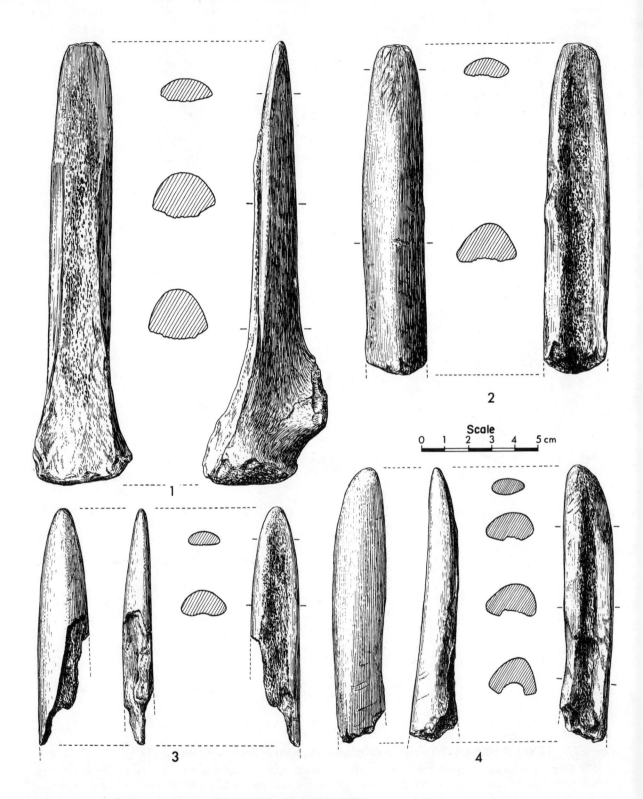

Figure 28.   LEVEL 3 ANTLER POLISHERS, OR *POLISSOIRS*

1 (296): Polisher of reindeer antler; 18.3 cm long. 2 (1284): Polisher of reindeer antler; 14 cm long. 3 (1536): Polisher of reindeer antler; 10 cm long; broken: distal portion. 4 (260): Polisher of reindeer antler; 11.5 cm long; broken: distal portion.

then been thinned from the interior side to form a tapering spatulate or bluntly rounded end. On most examples the cut (interior) side and the sides of the distal end have been smoothed and polished. Two examples on which this final stage is lacking clearly show the technique employed in the preceding stages (fig. 28, nos. 1, 4). One polisher made on the end of a naturally flat tine was simply bevelled and polished; the antler did not have to be split longitudinally to obtain the flattened profile.

Nine of the polishers are broken, only the distal end of the tool being present (fig. 28, nos. 3, 4). Another one may be complete (fig. 28, no. 2), but it cannot be ascertained whether the proximal end is cut or broken. Two examples are certainly complete (fig. 28, no. 1), preserving at the proximal end the articulation of the antler with the skull. In both cases, the tine near the articulation has been removed; one is broken off (the illustrated example), and the other is cut off. There is, finally, one former polisher, scored and snapped off at a point 58 mm behind the distal tip and split longitudinally by the groove-and-splinter technique.

Antler polishers are very poorly represented in Level 5, but those that are present are comparable to the Level 3 series.

Bone Smoothers (*Lissoirs*)

The majority of the bone smoothers are made from ribs; the use of this bone gives smoothers curved profiles if it is sufficiently long. One complete piece (fig. 29, no. 2) has the articulation of the rib with the vertebra preserved at the proximal end. The distal end of the tool is present on eight examples; on two it is broad and spatulate, and on others the sides constrict slightly to a very rounded point (fig. 29, nos. 1, 3, 5). The size of the pieces varies greatly, from a fragment over 280 mm long and about 22 mm wide (fig. 29, no. 1) to another fragment, probably almost complete, 82 mm long and only 9 mm wide.

Bone smoothers are virtually absent in Level 5, and the large variety characteristic of Level 3 is not represented at all.

Antler Smoothers (*Lissoirs*)

Smoothers made of antler are much less common than those made of bone, but at least two clear examples do exist. One is the bluntly pointed tip of a very large tool (fig. 29, no. 4), and the other is a tip fragment from a much smaller piece. Another piece of worked antler can be considered a crude smoother (*lissoir fruste*) or one in the course of manufacture; the characteristic distal end is roughed out, but behind that the sides still show the traces of removal from the shaft by the groove-and-splinter technique. The fourth piece is a small segment, probably of a smoother.

There are no antler smoothers in Level 5.

Ivory Smoother (*Lissoir*)

One fragmentary ivory smoother in a very poor state of preservation was found in Level 3. It is a distal tip, somewhat over 60 mm long, 20 mm wide, and 10 mm thick. It has a bluntly rounded point and a flattened, subrectangular section.

Bone Awls (*Poinçons* or *Alênes*)

Awls are among the most frequent bone artifacts in Level 3, but they do not form a tightly patterned series. The piercing tip, itself quite well made, has usually been created on an otherwise minimally modified bone fragment. There is wide variation in the diameter—and therefore the functional acuity—of the piercing tip. Some of the tips are quite small and delicate, having been set off from the shaft of the tool by a pronounced constriction or shoulder (fig. 30, nos. 6, 10). On other examples, the piercing tip is larger and sturdier, and the diameter increases evenly from the point toward the unmodified shaft (fig. 30, nos. 13, 14; fig. 31, no. 11). Crude awls (*poinçons frustes*), minimally modified but bearing signs of use, are also present (fig. 30, no. 11).

Antler Awls (*Poinçons* or *Alênes*)

There are only two antler awls in Level 3, both with long, well-made piercing tips but unfinished butt regions (fig. 30, no. 8).

Bone, Antler, and Ivory Sagaies

Level 3 produced a rich and varied series of sagaies (a loan-word from French used here to refer to the point or armature—made of organic material—of the kind of spear or lance known in English as an "assegai"). There are two major and several minor morphological variants that cross-cut the different categories of material. The variants are here described globally, with indication of how many are made of each material.

The most numerous (n=16) kind of sagaie in Level 3 is long, slender, and curved, with a subcircular section (fig. 31, nos. 1–3, 7). The point is sharp and usually quite round, but it may be formed by the intersection of flat, bevelled facets (fig. 31, no. 6). On four examples (three of antler and one of bone), the central part of the convexly curved side bears short transverse incisions; the base curves out opposite the side that is incised. With reference to similar pieces found in the Périgordian VI and Aurignacian V horizons at Laugerie-Haute, the Peyronys (D. Peyrony and E. Peyrony 1938; p. 23) suggested that the incised central section was attached to a bevelled haft in such a fashion that the outwardly curving base of the sagaie functioned as a barb. The base of this kind of sagaie may be rather sharply pointed (fig. 31, no. 1), more bluntly pointed (fig. 31, no. 4), formed into a roughly conical end by crude cutting (fig. 31, no. 2), or formed by the intersection of flat, bevelling facets, as also noted for the point (fig. 31, no. 5). Two fragmentary pieces with different base treatments probably represent examples of this kind of sagaie. One large fragment of antler has a well-formed, conical base scored all around by shallow transverse incisions (fig. 30, no. 3). A smaller piece, of bone, has a pronounced single bevel (fig. 30, no. 5). Unfortunately, there are no complete sagaies of this variant that have these base treatments. Of the 16 sagaies of the long, slender, curved kind, 11 are of antler, five are of bone, and none is of ivory. The largest examples are antler (fig. 31, no. 5; fig. 30, no. 3); the smallest examples are in both antler (fig. 31, no. 4) and bone (fig. 31, no. 6).

The next most numerous (n=11) kind of sagaie is shorter

and broader, with a straight profile and a subrectangular section (fig. 31, no. 10; fig. 30, no. 2). The point is again quite sharp, and the working of the point has given a subround section to the distal tip. One or both sides of the central region are flat (the antler examples show burin-cut grooves). On two of the ivory examples with only one flat side, this facet bears fine, parallel, transverse incisions (fig. 30, no. 2). None of the three complete antler examples are incised, but there are two antler segments of the appropriate size and subrectangular section that have flat, incised facets. The base

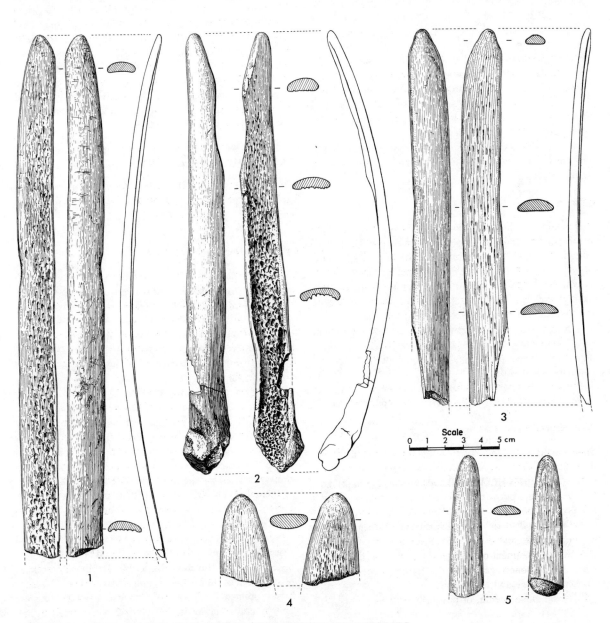

Figure 29.   LEVEL 3 BONE AND ANTLER SMOOTHERS, OR *LISSOIRS*

1 (230): Bone smoother; 28 cm long; proximal end broken. 2 (1955): Bone smoother; 23 cm long. 3 (221): Bone smoother; 20.5 cm long; proximal end broken. 4 (1939): Extreme distal portion of a smoother of reindeer antler. 5 (4208): Distal portion of a bone smoother.

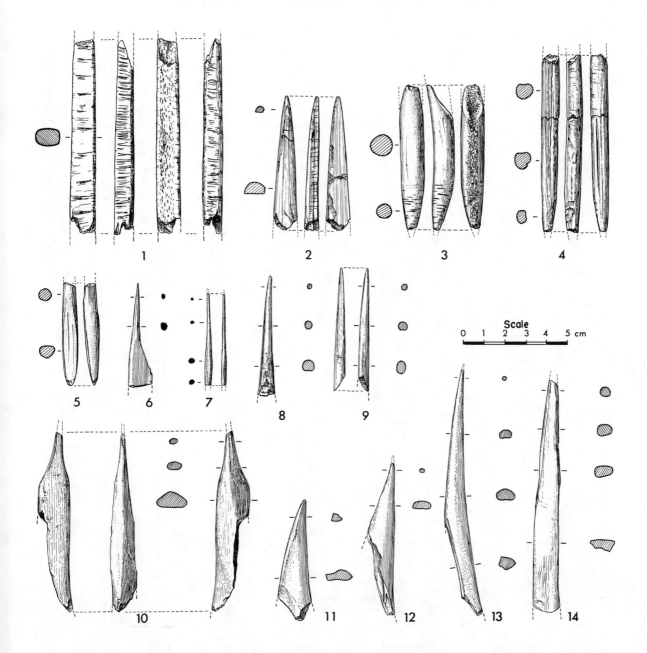

Figure 30.   LEVEL 3 BONE, ANTLER, AND IVORY TOOLS AND WEAPONS

1   (1263): Segment of reindeer antler *baguette* with subrectangular section; heavily incised with roughly parallel lines on three sides.

2   (1133): Ivory sagaie split longitudinally and incised with roughly parallel lines on one side; proximal extremity broken.

3   (2061): Sagaie of reindeer antler with transverse incisions on base; both extremities broken.

4   (1465): Segment of sagaie of reindeer antler with two opposing grooves; both extremities broken.

5   (2946): Bone sagaie with singly bevelled base; distal extremity broken.

6   (108): Bone awl, or *poinçon*; proximal extremity broken.

7   (115): Bone needle, or pin; both extremities broken.

8   (1744): Antler awl, or *poinçon*; proximal extremity broken.

9   (2802): Antler sagaie, or ? point; proximal portion broken.

10   (233): Large bone awl, or *poinçon*; both extremities broken.

11   (1727): Crude bone awl (*poinçon fruste*); proximal portion broken.

12   (544): Bone awl, or *poinçon*; proximal portion broken.

13   (1429): Very large bone awl, or *poinçon*; proximal extremity broken.

14   (99): Very large bone awl, or *poinçon*; both extremities broken.

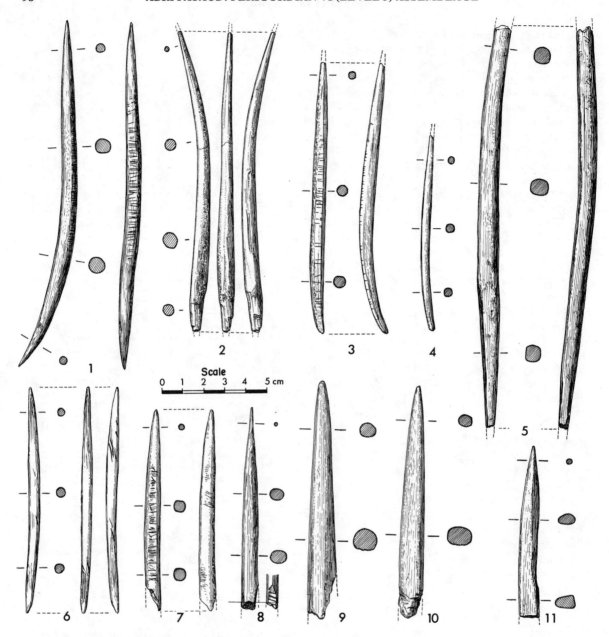

Figure 31. LEVEL 3 BONE AND ANTLER SAGAIES AND BONE AWL

1 (4303+4438): Curved sagaie of reindeer antler with roughly parallel incisions along one side (16.1 cm long).
2 (1983): Curved sagaie of reindeer antler (13.7 cm long); both extremities broken.
3 (1840): Curved sagaie of reindeer antler with roughly parallel incisions along one side (12.3 cm long).
4 (1068): Slightly curved small sagaie of bone with broken distal extremity (8.9 cm long).
5 (188): Slightly curved sagaie of reindeer antler with doubly bevelled base (18.4 cm long); both extremities broken.
6 (1537): Bone sagaie with diagonal incisions.
7 (2741): Sagaie of reindeer antler with roughly parallel incisions along one side; proximal extremity broken.
8 (137): Bone sagaie with laterally bevelled and incised base; proximal extremity broken.
9 (1131): Sagaie of reindeer antler (11 cm long); proximal extremity broken.
10 (2026+4968): Sagaie of reindeer antler with crudely conical, slightly broken base.
11 (1101): Bone awl, or *poinçon* (7.8 cm long); proximal extremity broken.

of this kind of sagaie, whether of antler (fig. 31, no. 10), bone, or ivory, is always roughly hacked or cut into a crude subconical form. A total of seven examples bear this base treatment. The short, broad, straight sagaie is represented by six examples of antler, one of bone, and six of ivory, and its size range is more uniform than that of the long, narrow, curved kind. The smallest examples, all of ivory and all fragmentary, would probably have had an original complete length of approximately 70 mm.

A third kind of sagaie is represented by three antler pieces, all distal extremities (fig. 31, no. 9). The profile is not curved, the sides are straight and tapering, and the section is subcircular. None of the examples bear incisions; the nature of the base is unknown. One fragmentary ivory example may be of this kind. The total length (99 mm) is preserved, but the sagaie is split longitudinally along the laminar structure in such a way that less than one-half the piece is present. The cross-section is almost certainly subcircular, and the base is clearly of the crudely cut, subconical variety.

A fourth kind of sagaie is long, slender, and straight with a suboval cross-section; the central portion is neither faceted nor incised. The very distinctive base has a *side* bevel bearing fine transverse incisions. (This kind of sagaie is very different from the piece referred to above that has a single bevelled base and that probably belongs to the first kind of sagaie.) In Level 3, there are two almost complete specimens—one of antler and one of bone (fig. 31, no. 8)—of the suboval, side-bevelled sagaies, plus a long antler segment that is very probably of this same variety.

The fifth and final kind of sagaie is represented by two fragments of antler (fig. 30, no. 4). The section is roughly plano-convex. The distinctive feature is a groove (*cannelure*) present on one or, in the case of the illustrated piece, two surfaces. The extremity treatment cannot be characterized from the sample available.

To recapitulate, in Level 3 there are five distinctive kinds of sagaies made of three different materials, as follows:

	Antler	Bone	Ivory	Total
Long, slender, *curved,* subcircular section	11	5	—	16
Short, broad, straight, subrectangular section, *conical base*	6	1	6	13
Long, slender, *straight,* subcircular section	3	—	1?	4
Long, slender, straight, *suboval section, side bevel*	2	1	—	3
Straight, plano-convex section, *grooved*	2	—	—	2

Sagaies of any kind are so rare and indefinite in Level 5 that no detailed comparison wth the Level 3 series can be made. Indeed, the most meaningful comparative statement is that there is here a major difference between the two assemblages. The rich and varied series of bone, antler, and ivory sagaies in the Périgordian VI of Level 3 is not found in the Périgordian IV series of Level 5; furthermore, the former cannot be seen as developing from the latter.

Bone Gorges (*Hameçons*)

Gorges are small, bipointed bone objects believed to be fishing equipment. All of the gorges in Level 3 are doubtful examples. Three of them (fig. 27, no. 10) have a tapering point at one end and a cut constriction terminating in a break at the other end. Although they may be something quite different, they may also be one broken half of a gorge constricted in the middle to permit attachment of the line. The other piece (33 mm long and approximately 3 mm in diameter) has a rather sharp point at one end and a very blunt point at the other. The middle shows no constriction or swelling.

Bone Pin

The one bone pin in Level 3 has a bulbous head that has been carefully worked and separated from the shaft of the pin by a slight constriction (fig. 27, no. 11).

Eyeless Bone Needle or Pin

The eyeless bone needle or pin (fig. 30, no. 7) has a long and extremely fine shaft well degaged from the thicker butt of the tool. The distal 4 to 5 mm of the needle are charred, and the extreme point is broken or burnt away.

Bone Flaking Tools or Anvils (*Compresseurs*)

Four fragments of bone—three long bones and one rib—have somewhere on their edges or flat surfaces multiple cuts, scratches, and abrasions resulting from use as a flaking tool or compressor. None of them shows concave areas of intensive pitting and battering (resulting from use as an anvil) like those found on thicker and heavier fragments of bone in Level 5. One of the long bone fragments shows evidence that after its use as a flaking tool it was extensively gnawed by an animal.

Antler Wedge (*Coin*)

In Level 3, there are no bone wedges like the several very clear examples in Level 5, but one fragment of antler shaft (fig. 32, no. 3) was probably used in the same way.

Fusiform Bone Object

This object is 55 mm long and has a rounded section with a slightly flattened base (fig. 27, no. 9). One end is pointed, and the other is constricted to form a head, apparently for the attachment of a line. The piece cannot be seen as a gorge, and it may well have served as a suspended ornament.

Antler "*Baguettes*"

The so-called *baguettes* are straight-sided, flat-profile rods or wands made from shafts of reindeer antler. The section ranges from subrectangular to flattened oval, depending on how much rounding or finishing was done after the piece had been separated from the shaft by the groove-and-splinter technique. All three examples are fragmentary, but the largest one (167 mm long) ends in a well-worked, tapering, blunt point. One of the two *baguette* segments (fig. 30, no. 1) has multiple transverse incised or engraved lines on the upper surface and both sides. The cross-section of this piece is also interesting; one side has been extensively rounded and finished after its removal from the parent shaft, but the other side has been minimally modified and the face of the burin-cut groove is still clearly visible. The function of these *baguettes* is unknown, but it is at least possible that they were weapon armatures. There are no similar pieces in Level 5.

Incised Bone

Five fragments of bone in Level 3 bear regular, intentionally incised lines. One piece of a small rib (fig. 26, no. 2) has two strongly incised parallel lines and several fainter ones. A fragment of a much larger rib (fig. 26, no. 1) is covered on one surface by a sort of crosshatch design.

Antler Cut by Groove-and-Splinter Technique

Most of these objects are pieces of antler detached longitudinally from the body of the shaft by two burin-cut grooves extending from the surface into the spongy tissue. One of them has been subsequently gnawed by an animal. On some examples (fig. 32, nos. 1, 4), additional grooves for further dividing the antler have been roughed out or started on the outer surface. Two pieces show quite clearly the method of removing unwanted tines from the body of the shaft. On one, a deep groove has been cut parallel to the shaft at the shaft-tine junction. The other piece is a removed tine with two deep, almost intersecting grooves, one made from each surface. Such removed tines are well represented in Level 5.

Two pieces of antler (neither of which is illustrated) seem to indicate an alternative technique for dividing the shaft into convenient pieces. A burin has been used to cut a very short groove (40 to 50 mm long) somewhere near the middle of the shaft. The piece in its present form is split along the axis of the groove. Presumably the short groove provided a placed for the insertion of a wedge, which was then driven in to split the antler. One antler polisher (fig. 28, no. 4) seems to have been split in this fashion.

Miscellaneous Worked Bone

Included in this residual category are fragmentary or slightly worked pieces that cannot be included in any more formal category. Two pieces are of particular interest:

a. A tympanic bone, probably of reindeer, bearing miscellaneous cuts and scratches.
b. A short (49 mm) bipointed splinter of bone formed by the intersection of two natural fractures. Both pointed ends are very sharp, and one has been slightly modified to increase its acuity. The only other modifications are many fine scratches on the outer surface of the bone at both pointed ends. A large series of such pieces was illustrated from the site of La Gravette by Lacorre (1960, p. 315, pl. LXXXIV, nos. 4–6, 16, 17) as possible gorges (*hameçons*).

Miscellaneous Worked Antler

This is a residual category containing unfinished or fragmentary tools. Also included are two antler shafts that have been divided transversely by cutting or chopping through the whole circumference of the hard outer layer and snapping the rest.

Miscellaneous Worked Ivory

There are only two miscellaneous pieces of worked ivory, both split longitudinally along the laminar structure. The first is an elongate, rodlike object (90 mm long) that has a broken surface at one end and a flattened, knoblike protrusion at the other. The second piece is a long, thin flake; the original piece probably had a rounded section, but too little is preserved to permit its identification as a sagaie or other tool.

SUMMARY AND CONCLUSIONS

Artifacts of stone other than flint are not frequent in Level 3; with the exception of coloring matter, this is true also of Level 5. A major difference between the levels occurs in the frequency and use of hematite. Although areas of Level 3 were heavily stained red by powdered ochre, comparatively few actual fragments of hematite were found. In various

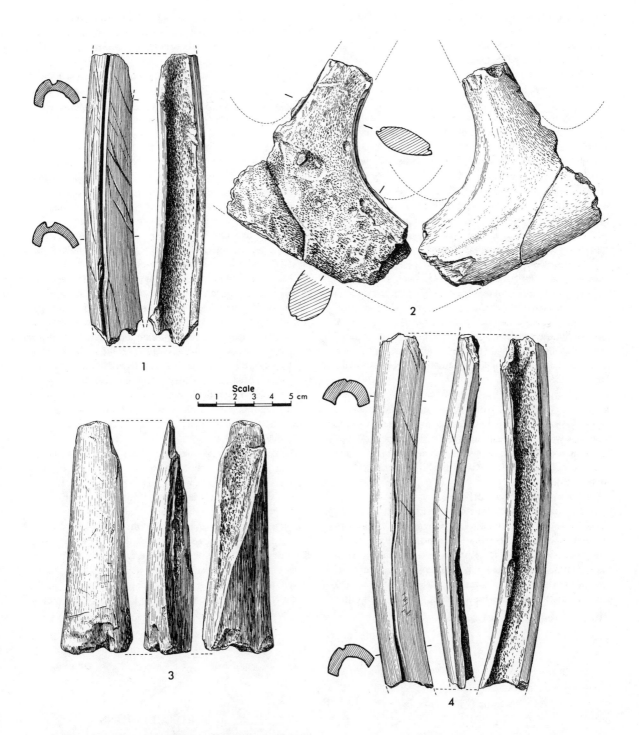

Figure 32. LEVEL 3 WORKED ANTLER OBJECTS

1 (2341): Reindeer antler segment with diagonal incisions executed prior to cutting by groove-and-splinter technique. Note: *Ébauche* of groove on upper surface.

2 (1352): Reindeer antler débitage cut in circular fashion by groove-and-splinter technique.

3 (622): Reindeer antler wedge (coin) with natural breaks at proximal extremity and along one side.

4 (2790): Reindeer antler segment cut by groove-and-splinter technique. Note *Ébauche* of groove on upper surface.

lenses of Level 5 that were also stained red, discrete hematite fragments were very numerous. Some of the hematite fragments in Level 3 were rubbed or ground against a hard substance, producing faceted and striated crayons. With one exception, this technique seems not to have been used in Level 5, where the ochre was presumably powdered by crushing.

The presence of detached stone art objects (*art mobilier*) in Level 3 is a distinctive feature of the cultural inventory that contrasts with that of Level 5, from which such art is absent.

With the exception of these differences, the objects made of stone other than flint in Levels 3 and 5 are very similar. None, however, is very distinctive, and no far-reaching cultural conclusions can be drawn from the comparison.

The importation into the site of marine and other exotic shells for use as ornaments was not of great quantitative importance during either the Level 3 or Level 5 occupation.

The industry of tooth, bone, antler, and ivory in Level 3 is characterized primarily by its richness and variation. It contrasts very markedly with that of Level 5, which is very poor in all but objects of personal adornment. On the other hand, objects of personal adornment are not numerous in Level 3; specifically, the squash-seed variety of bone pendant found throughout the thickness of Level 5 (and present also at La Gravette) is absent from the Périgordian VI of Level 3 at the Abri Pataud.

A large proportion of the bone, antler, and ivory artifacts in Level 3 are sagaies of several different sizes and morphologies. The use of these organic materials for weapon armatures was not of great quantitative importance in Level 5, and the several sagaies or possible sagaies in Level 5 do not have analogues in the larger and much more standardized Level 3 series.

Fishing tackle in the form of bone gorges is only doubtfully present in Level 3; this is true also for Level 5.

The bone and antler tools of unknown function that are called polishers and smoothers occur in Level 3 in a large, patterned series. Several less standardized polishers occur in Level 5, but smoothers are almost absent. Awls, mainly of bone, are frequent in both Levels 5 and 3, and because of the usual simplicity of these tools, many generic similarities exist.

Bone or antler tools or weapons with incised decoration occur both in Level 3 (antler *baguettes*) and in Level 5 (bone awls), but they are very rare in both. Neither level has yielded engraved bone art objects.

Manufacturing byproducts, especially fragments of antler cut by the groove-and-splinter technique, are present but nondistinctive in both levels.

The differences between the nonflint industries of Levels 3 and 5 are great, but they often consist of frequency differences—the rich variety of the Périgordian VI pieces contrasted with the poverty of those in the Périgordian IV. Because the state of preservation of bone and antler in both levels is excellent, the quantitative difference cannot be explained as an accident of preservation. Nor is sampling error a likely factor, because the total Level 5 assemblage is much larger than that of Level 3. The different frequencies of nonflint artifacts, particularly bone and antler, in the two levels is real and must derive from economic and/or traditional considerations. That some differences in traditions of tool manufacture and use are involved can be seen from a qualitative comparison of the two series. Statements about cultural similarity and difference have long been based on the typology of sagaies; on this criterion alone, no relationship whatsoever can be seen between Level 3 and Level 5. Other differences—ones that are more difficult to assess—are, however, present. These include differences in the use of coloring matter, in articles of personal adornment, and in the more banal bone and antler tools. Points of similarity between the levels are limited to generic likenesses in banal, nonelaborated objects.

The similarity and continuity between the Périgordian IV and Périgordian VI at the Abri Pataud are shown convincingly and repeatedly by the various tool classes of the flint industry. The nonflint industry offers no support for this view but emphasizes instead discontinuity and difference. Some changes and new elements between the Périgordian IV and Périgordian VI were visible in the flint tools, but these changes are best represented in the nonflint industry. Although in many important ways the Périgordian IV and the Périgordian VI represent different stages in a continuing cultural tradition, the bone and antler industry is not a part of this evolving continuity.

X

The Level 3 Assemblage: Summary and Discussion

THE FLINT INDUSTRY

Scrapers are far less numerous than burins in the Level 3 assemblage. Although most of the scrapers are end-scrapers, there is an extensive series of scrapers of other kinds as well. The end-scrapers are best considered as a unitary tool class; they are not divisible into natural subgroups based on attribute clustering. The arc-of-circle contour is most common, followed by asymmetrical and irregular contours. The great majority are made on blades with either very regular parallel sides or, often, a completely nonrectilinear blank contour. Although a triangular blank cross-section is most common, the majority of scraping edges have a non-convergent retouch pattern. Marginal retouch, mostly fine, is rare in the end-scraper sample. The scrapers on amorphous flakes, characterized by the ocurrence of a very regular end-scraper–like edge on an amorphous flake blank, are a distinctive element of the Level 3 assemblage. There are also circular scrapers on flakes, but these are not the *coupoirs* known from later Level 5 and other Périgordian IV assemblages. Asymmetrical knives are present but rare.

Backed tools are very numerous in Level 3. Most of them are Gravette points, but *lamelles à dos tronquées* are also present. There are no Font-Robert points and no true *éléments tronqués*. The Level 3 Gravette points are divided into two subgroups, AB and C. The Gravettes of subgroup AB, constituting the majority of the sample, are best characterized as short, narrow, and spiky. Backing is predominantly heavy and bidirectional, and almost one-half of the pieces are backed on the left. The tool extremities are often unretouched, but on examples with retouched extremities, obverse retouch is frequent, especially at the point. Obverse retouch is important also on the edge opposite the backing. The frequent occurrence of Vachons retouch on the butt is a characteristic of the Level 3 Gravette point series. Most complete examples have a parallel- or subparallel-sided morphology; the Châtelperronoid form is absent. The segmented backed bladelet technique, characteristic of the Level 2 (Proto-Magdalenian) backed tool series, is also present in Level 3. The *lamelles à dos tronquées* produced by this technique are rare in Level 3, but they occur with the same distinctive distal and proximal byproducts that are found in Level 2. Nevertheless, use of the segmented backed bladelet technique apparently played a very minor role in the Level 3 tool-making tradition.

Burins are very numerous in Level 3, accounting for approximately one-third of the total graphed flint industry.

They are predominantly truncation burins, often double or multiple, and other kinds of burins tend to approach truncation burin norms in their attribute distributions. The truncation burins are usually made on blades, rarely with marginal retouch, and most have straight or bevelled edges. The burin removals are very often canted toward the ventral surface, and the SRS is predominantly concave and oblique; these dispositions of the burin removal and the SRS are seen as devices to increase the acuity of the burin edge. Among the small truncation burins are two that, although they lack stop-notches, can be called Noailles burins. A small series of transverse burins on notched flakes is a distinctive characteristic of the Level 3 burin series; these are either truncation burins or retouched edge burins. There are two distinct subtypes of dihedral burins—"median" and "lateral"—based on the position of the burin edge relative to the working axis of the blank. The "median" dihedral burins are generally sharper and have thicker burin edges, whereas the "lateral" dihedral burins are more like truncation and break burins in their major attributes. The segmentation of the dihedral burin series, doubtless reflecting functional differentiation, is a characteristic of the Level 3 burin series. Break burins have attribute distributions similar to those of truncation burins.

Truncated pieces in Level 3 are clearly a functionally heterogeneous class. The most important tool type within the class is the "truncation borer," a perforating tool manufactured using the truncation technique. Such pieces were important to Peyrony's original characterization of his "Périgordian III" from Laugerie-Haute (D. Peyrony 1933; D. Peyrony and E. Peyrony 1938). Other kinds of truncated pieces are unstruck burins and concave scrapers.

Most of the Level 3 nuclei are prismatic, and many have two opposed striking platforms. The overwhelming majority of nuclei are of local Campanian or Coniacian flint. The exotic Maestrichtian flint, rare in the nucleus sample, is better represented among the retouched tools; this suggests that some of the tools were made elsewhere and brought to the Abri Pataud in finished form.

THE NONFLINT INDUSTRY

An important characteristic of the Level 3 assemblage is the richness of its nonflint industry. Tools and weapons of bone, antler, and ivory are particularly numerous. The occurrence of objects of personal adornment is more limited. The principal components of the nonflint industry are summarized in the paragraphs below.

There is in Level 3 a good series of tools presumably used in the flint-knapping process. These include hammerstones, stone *retouchoirs,* and bone *compresseurs.* Objects of personal adornment, which are varied although not numerous, include peforated teeth and mollusc shells. Some of the fossil shells come from the local limestone, and some come from Miocene deposits of the Bordeaux region. All of the Pleistocene marine molluscs but one are from the Atlantic coast of France; the exception is one species that may have come from either the Atlantic or the Mediterranean. The five flint *pendeloques* included in the graphed assemblage are presumably also objects of personal adornment. The red ochre crayons and other coloring matter found in Level 3 may have been used both for body ornamentation and for the production of mural or other art.

Sagaies of bone, antler, and ivory comprise an important part of the nonflint industry. Five different varieties are recognized, of which the most numerous and characteristic are: a) a long, slender, curved variety with subcircular section, and b) a short, broad, straight variety with subrectangular section and conical base. Polishers, smoothers and awls are well represented, and there is a small series of antler *baguettes* with subrectangular or oval section.

ART

Vestiges of art are numerous in Level 3 and the overlying *éboulis,* and a strong artistic development is one of the major characteristics of the Périgordian VI as it is known from the Abri Pataud. The various manifestations of art in Level 3 have been discussed elsewhere by Movius (1977, pp. 47–53), and only a brief summary is presented here.

The most important art object from this horizon is a Venus figure, a bas-relief carving of a young female made on a small tabular fragment of limestone. This object, belonging to the widespread tradition of Upper Palaeolithic Venuses, is almost certainly from Level 3, but its exact stratigraphic provenience is unknown. Other mobilary art from Level 3 includes two engraved pebbles of dolomitic limestone, one of which has been used as an anvil stone.

A very large series (several hundred fragments) of engraved and/or painted limestone plaques were found in association with the Level 3 occupation. Some came to light within the major occupation horizon, but the great majority were from the base of Eboulis 2-3 at the rear of the shelter. At least one of the very large limestone blocks that formed the front limit of the "long-house" habitation area in Lens 2 bore an engraving. Weathering and disintegration of the limestone walls has reduced most of the Level 3 mural art to completely indecipherable fragments. It is clear, however, that at the time of the Level 3 occupation much of the back wall and roof of the shelter must have been decorated. Although the content of this art can rarely be deciphered, the techniques employed include bas-relief carving, shallow engraving, and the application of red, black, and white paint.

COMPARISONS

A general comparative study of the Périgordian VI In the Les Eyzies vicinity has been made by Clay (1968, 1976). Based on assemblage samples from both the Abri Pataud and Laugerie-Haute, it is part of his detailed investigation of previously suggested relationships between the Périgordian and Proto-Magdalenian tool-making traditions. Because a summary of his findings will be presented in a later volume of this series, we mention here only Clay's general conclusion that the assemblages of Pataud: 3 and Laugerie-Haute: Est: B and B' can be considered to represent a single archaeological phase. There are great similarities among these three assemblages (fig. 33)[6], but, on the basis of the differences that exist, Clay reconizes two sequential subphases—an Early Périgordian VI (Pataud: 3) and a Late Périgordian VI (Laugerie-Haute: Est: B and B').

Throughout this present study, comparison has frequently been made between the Level 3 assemblage and those of Level 5 (Bricker 1973), particularly the later units of Level 5 (the Périgordian IV proper). The tool-class frequencies are similar, as shown by the cumulative graphs, but in Level 3 there are proportionally fewer end-scrapers, more burins, and fewer marginally retouched pieces. The blanks on which end-scrapers are made in Level 3 differ somewhat from those in later Level 5, but the scraping edges themselves are very similar. Asymmetrical knives are present in both levels, but the *coupoirs* of the Périgordian IV are absent from the Périgordian VI. The Gravette points of Level 3 are quite similar to those of later Level 5, and, even more important, they continue several trends of change through time established within Level 5. The segmented backed bladelet technique, absent in Level 5, appears as a new element in Level 3. The burin series of Level 3 differs from that of later Level 5 in two major respects: a) the segregation of dihedral burins into "median" and "lateral" varieties, and b) the greatly increased proportion of truncation burins. In other ways, the series are similar, and, as is the case with Gravette points, the burins of Level 3 continue trends of change through time visible in Level 5. The major difference between the Périgordian VI and the Périgordian IV occurs in the nonflint industry. The richness of the Périgordian VI, particularly in objects of bone and antler, is completely new, a characteristic scarcely suggested by the situation in the Périgordian IV. The same is true of the artistic development of the Périgordian VI. These differences are, however, overshadowed by the similarities in the flint industries of the two levels—similarities that attest to a direct continuity of technological tradition between the Périgordian IV and the Périgordian VI.

---

6. Information needed to draw the graphs for Laugerie-Haute: Est: B and B' comes from two sources. The type count of the backed tools was done at the Musée Nationale de Préhistoire in Les Eyzies by H. L. Movius, Jr., and H. M. Bricker. Type counts of other tools were taken from information published by de Sonneville-Bordes (1960, pp. 259, 260, tableau XXI).

Detailed comparisons between the Level 3 assemblage and those of Level 4 (Noaillian) have been made by David (1966), and a summary of his findings will be presented in a later volume of this series. Both the Level 3 and Level 5 assemblages differ from those of Level 4 in virtually all respects—tool-class frequencies as well as typological and technological details. Only two similarities can be recognized between the Périgordian VI and the Noaillian: a) in both, truncation burins, often multiple, are far more numerous than dihedral burins, and b) both have rich nonflint industries. The presence of two Noailles burins in Level 3 has no great culture-historical significance; it very easily could be no more than an example of typological convergence within the large and varied Périgordian VI truncation burin

sample. The Noaillian tool-making tradition is very different from that represented by the Périgordian IV and VI, and it is not possible to consider the Noaillian as the tool-making tradition from which the Périgordian VI developed.

As mentioned above, the relationship between the Périgordian VI and the Proto-Magdalenian has been studied by Clay (ibid), and his results will be presented in a later volume of this series. However, it is necessary here to point out that in the assemblages there is only one similarity that would argue for a close relationship between the Périgordian VI and the Proto-Magdalenian—namely, the segmented backed bladelet technique, which is present in both. With this exception, nothing suggests that Périgordian VI and Proto-Magdalenian tools are products of the same tool-making

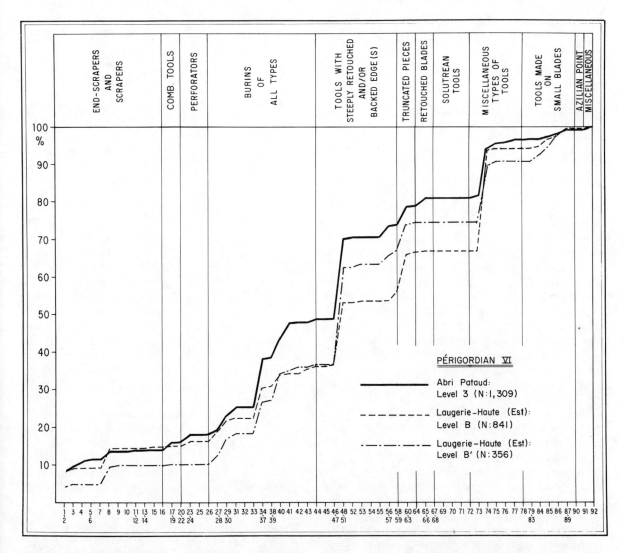

Figure 33. CUMULATIVE GRAPHS FOR THE ASSEMBLAGE SAMPLES FROM ABRI PATAUD: LEVEL 3 (SOLID LINE), LAUGERIE-HAUTE EST: LEVEL B (DASHED LINE), AND LAUGERIE-HAUTE EST: LEVEL B′ (INTERRUPTED LINE).

tradition, whatever name such a tradition may be given. Certainly there is no convincing evidence that the Périgordian VI is in any meaningful way ancestral to the Proto-Magdalenian.

In summary, the results of this present study and of others indicate that the Level 3 (Périgordian VI) assemblage has no close relationships with either the Noaillian or the Proto-Magdalenian. Its closest resemblances are with later Level 5 (Périgordian IV). The Périgordian IV and VI are not identical, but we do not consider that the differences are greater in any respect than those that may reasonably be expected to occur over a period of approximately 5,000 years through the internal evolution of a single cultural tradition.

References

Bouchud, Jean
  1966   *Essai sur le renne et la climatologie du Paléolithique moyen et supérieur.* Périgueux, Imprimerie Magne.
  1975   "Etude de la faune de l'abri Pataud," in *Excavation of the Abri Pataud, Les Eyzies (Dordogne),* H. L. Movius, Jr., ed., American School of Prehistoric Research, Bulletin no. 30, pp. 69–153. Peabody Museum, Harvard University.

Bourlon, Maurice
  1911   "Essai de classification des burins. Leurs modes d'avivage," *Revue Anthropologique,* vol. 21, pp. 267–278.

Bricker, Harvey M.
  1973   "The Périgordian IV and Related Cultures in France." Ph.D. dissertation, Harvard University.
  1976   "La contribution de l'Abri Pataud á la question bayacienne," *Congrès Préhistorique de France, Comptes Rendus de la XXe Session, Provence, 1974,* pp. 48–52. Issoudun, Imprimerie Laboureur.
  1978   "Lower to Middle Périgordian Continuity," in *Codex Wauchope (Human Mosaic,* vol. 12), M. J. Giardino et al., eds., pp. 165–182. New Orleans, Human Mosaic.

Brooks, Alison S.
  1979   "The Significance of Variability in Palaeolithic Assemblages: An Aurignacian Example from Southwestern France." Ph.D. dissertation, Harvard University.

Cheynier, André
  1962   "Le Cirque de la Patrie. Déscription des outillages." *Mémoire de la Société Préhistorique Française,* no. 6, pp. 61–173.

Clay, R. Berle
  1968   "The Proto-Magdalenian Culture." Ph.D. dissertation, Southern Illinois University.
  1975   "Concerning the Spatial Analysis of Occupation Floors," *American Antiquity,* vol. 40, pp. 357–358.

  1976   "Typological Classification, Attribute Analysis, and Lithic Variability," *Journal of Field Archaeology,* vol. 3, pp. 303–311.

Collins, Michael B.
  n.d.a.   "A Preliminary Examination of the Evidence for Heat Treating of Raysse Burins from the Abri Pataud (Dordogne) France." Unpublished manuscript.
  n.d.b.   "Lithic Technology at Laugerie Haute and the Abri Pataud, France." Paper presented in the symposium "Recent Research on the European Palaeolithic," 40th Annual Meeting of the Society for American Archaeology, Dallas, Texas, May 8, 1975.

Dance, S. Peter
  1975   "The Molluscan Fauna," in *Excavation of the Abri Pataud, Les Eyzies (Dordogne),* H. L. Movius, Jr., ed., American School of Prehistoric Research, Bulletin no. 30, pp. 154–159. Peabody Museum, Harvard University.

David, Nicholas
  1966   "The Périgordian Vc: An Upper Palaeolithic Culture in Western Europe." Ph.D. dissertation, Harvard University.
  1973   "On Upper Palaeolithic Society, Ecology, and Technological Change: The Noaillian Case," in *The Explanation of Culture Change: Models in Prehistory,* C. Renfrew, ed., pp. 277–303. Pittsburgh, University of Pittsburgh Press.

Donner, Joakim J.
  1975   "Pollen Composition of the Abri Pataud Sediments," in *Excavation of the Abri Pataud, Les Eyzies (Dordogne),* H. L. Movius, Jr., ed., American School of Prehistoric Research, Bulletin no. 30, pp. 160–173. Peabody Museum, Harvard University.

Farrand, William R.
  1975   "Analysis of the Abri Pataud Sediments," in *Excavation of the Abri Pataud, Les Eyzies (Dordogne),* H. L. Movius, Jr., ed., American School of Prehistoric Research, Bulletin no. 30, pp. 27–68. Peabody Museum, Harvard University.

Lacorre, Fernand
1960   *La Gravette. Le Gravétien et le Bayacien.*
Laval, Imprimerie Barnéoud S. A.

Laville, Henri
1975   *Climatologie et chronologie du Paléolithique en Périgord: Etude sédimentologique de dépôts en grottes et sous abris.* Etudes Quaternaires, Mémoire no. 4. Laboratoire de Paléontologie Humaine et de Préhistoire, Université de Provence.

Movius, Hallam L., Jr.
1968   "Segmented Backed Bladelets," *Quartär,* vol. 19, pp. 239–249.
1974   "The Abri Pataud Program of the French Upper Paleolithic in Retrospect," in *Archaeological Researches in Retrospect,* G. R. Willey, ed., pp. 87–116. Cambridge, Winthrop Publishers, Inc.
1977   *Excavation of the Abri Pataud, Les Eyzies (Dordogne): Stratigraphy.* American School of Prehistoric Research, Bulletin no. 31. Peabody Museum, Harvard University.

Movius, Hallam L., Jr., ed.
1975   *Excavation of the Abri Pataud, Les Eyzies (Dordogne).* American School of Prehistoric Research, Bulletin no. 30. Peabody Museum, Harvard University.

Movius, Hallam L., Jr., and Alison S. Brooks
1971   "The Analysis of Certain Major Classes of Upper Palaeolithic Tools: Aurignacian Scrapers," *Proceedings of the Prehistoric Society,* vol. 37, pp. 253–273.

Movius, Hallam L., Jr. and Nicholas C. David
1970   "Burins avec modification tertiaire du biseau, burins-pointe et burins du Raysse à l'abri Pataud, Les Eyzies (Dordogne)," *Bulletin de la Société Préhistorique Française,* vol. 67, pp. 445–455.

Movius, Hallam L., Jr., Nicholas C. David, Harvey M. Bricker, and R. Berle Clay
1968   *The Analysis of Certain Major Classes of Upper Palaeolithic Tools.* American School of Prehistoric Research, Bulletin no. 26. Peabody Museum, Harvard University.

Peyrony, Denis
1933   "Les industries 'aurignaciennes' dans le bassin de la Vézère," *Bulletin de la Société Préhistorique Française,* vol. 30, pp. 543–559.

1936   "Le Périgordien et l'Aurignacien (nouvelles obsérvations)," *Bulletin de la Société Préhistorique Française,* vol. 33, pp. 616–619.

Peyrony, Denis and Elie Peyrony
1938   *Laugerie-Haute.* Archives de l'Institut de Paléontologie Humaine, Mémoire no. 19. Paris, Masson et Cie.

Semenov, S. A.
1964   *Prehistoric Technology: An Experimental Study of the Oldest Tools and Artifacts from Traces of Manufacture and Wear,* M. W. Thompson, trans. Bath, Adams and Dart.

Sonneville-Bordes, Denise de
1954   "Esquisse d'une évolution typologique du Paléolithique supérieur en Périgord: défense et illustration de la méthode," *L'Anthropologie,* vol. 58, pp. 197–230.
1960   *Le Paléolithique supérieur en Périgord.* Bordeaux, Imprimeries Delmas.

Sonneville-Bordes, Denise de and Jean Perrot
1954–   "Lexique typologique du Paléolithique su-
1956   périeur. Outillage lithique," *Bulletin de la Société Préhistorique Française,* vol. 51, pp. 327–335; vol. 52, pp. 76–79; vol. 53, pp. 408–412, 547–549.

Spiess, Arthur E.
1979   *Reindeer and Caribou Hunters: An Archaeological Study.* New York, Academic Press.

Tixier, Jacques
1958   "Les burins de Noailles de l'abri André Ragout, Bois-du-Roc, Vilhonneur (Charente)," *Bulletin de la Société Préhistorique Française,* vol. 55, pp. 628–644.

Vértes, László
1964   "Die Ausgrabung und die archäologischen Funde," in *Tata: Eine mittelpaläolithische Travertin-Siedlung in Ungarn,* L. Vértes, ed., Archaeologia Hungarica, Series Nova, XLIII, pp. 133–249. Budapest, Akadémiai Kiàdó.

Vogel, J. C., and H. T. Waterbolk
1963   "Groningen Radiocarbon Dates IV," *Radiocarbon,* vol. 5, pp. 163–202.
1967   "Groningen Radiocarbon Dates VII," *Radiocarbon,* vol. 9, pp. 107–155.

Waterbolk, H. T.
  1971   "Working with Radiocarbon Dates," *Proceedings of the Prehistoric Society,* vol. 37, pt. 2, pp. 15–33.

Whallon, Robert, Jr.
  1973   "Spatial Analysis of Palaeolithic Occupation Areas," in *The Explanation of Culture Change: Models in Prehistory,* C. Renfrew, ed., pp. 115–130. Pittsburgh, University of Pittsburgh Press.
  1974   "Spatial Analysis of Occupation Floors II: The Application of Nearest Neighbor Analysis," *American Antiquity,* vol. 39, pp. 16–34.